goodenoughmothering

goodenough**mothering**

THE BEST OF THE BLOG

Elaine Heffner, LCSW, Ed.D

To order additional copies of this book, contact:
Xlibris Corporation
1-888-795-4274
www.Xlibris.com
Orders@Xlibris.com
118370

To all the parents who have taught me so much.

Acknowledgments

I want to thank Alice Wilder, who spurred the writing of my blog, encouraged me, and held my hand through my first baby steps in the world of technology. Thanks, too, to Kristian Stout, who has helped me function in that world and has been responsive unfailingly to all of my queries along the way.

Most of all, my enduring love and thanks to my husband, Richard Heffner, who tirelessly reads all of my material and inevitably makes the imperfect less so.

CONTENTS

Introduction

Good enough mothering. What does that mean? Why does it matter? Don't mothers think they are good enough?

In my experience as a parent educator and psychotherapist, I see mothers trying to be perfect. "Good enough" doesn't feel good enough. How did that happen? I started my blog for parents in order to have a conversation about this question, and about the many other questions mothers have asked me over the years. This book is a selection of earlier posts for those who may have missed them, or would like to have them for easy reference.

Let me start by saying that mothers' worries that they may not be doing a good enough job come, in part, from the children themselves. Children want you to be perfect (that is, to do whatever they want you to do and to make them happy all the time), but that doesn't mean you *should* be . . . . or that it would be *good for them* if you could be.

Perhaps, deep down inside we all wish life could have been perfect for us as children, and so we are too ready to agree with our children that we should be able to make life perfect for them. But we can't—and that makes us feel guilty. Feeling guilty seems to be a normal condition of motherhood. So let me assure you that *feeling* guilty does not mean you *are* guilty. Those feelings do not mean you are not doing a good enough job.

So, just what is "good enough?" To answer that question we have to think about the purpose of child-rearing: what our goal is as parents. We know children are dependent creatures who have to be taken care of—sometimes it seems forever. We know we must provide them with food, shelter and clothing. But we also have to prepare and teach them to live in the world they will live in. That means becoming self-sufficient, while at the same time knowing how to get along with others. They have to learn to meet their own needs while still considering the needs and wishes of others. This is the art of living. Teaching this to children is the art of mothering.

Unfortunately, a great deal of energy has gone into trying to turn this art into a science. Mothers too often try to be scientists raising perfect children. And the real purpose of child-rearing has gotten lost.

Children begin life not only dependent on adults for survival, but also with limited means of expression and self-control. They are primarily concerned with gratifying their own needs and wishes. As they grow and mature they will gradually acquire the skills they need to function independently while also learning to consider others. As parents, our role is to teach and guide them while they are learning.

Over the years, child development research has given rise to many theories about how mothers "should" do this job (for mostly the job has been assigned to mothers.) Several messages have been delivered through these theories:

One is that a good mother will put the needs of her child first.

A second is that not meeting a child's needs will be damaging to the child.

A third is that there is a right way and a wrong way of responding to a child, and that a child's development depends on doing it the "right" way. Doing it the "wrong" way can harm a child.

These messages have given mothers the idea that they have great potential for damaging their children. So mothers search for the "right" way to do things and think they must be to blame if there are any bumps on the developmental road.

But there are always going to be bumps . . . and mothers don't cause them. Nor do they mean you did something wrong. They are part of life and of learning to live in the real world.

We are going to look together at some of those bumps, think about what they tell us and how to help our children over them.

MOTHER WORRIES

Mothers' Guilt

Probably nothing plagues mothers as much as feelings of guilt about things they have done—or haven't done—to or for their children.

A father once said to me, "Guilt is not my thing." Unfortunately, it *does* seem to be a mother's "thing". One reason for that is the great sense of responsibility a mother feels for her child. Another is the power to influence children—both for good and for bad—that has been attributed to mothers, in child development research as well as in popular literature.

But perhaps a major source of guilt is the anger we sometimes feel that is provoked by children's behavior. Children really know how to push our buttons, and we're always struggling with their behavior that gets to us the most. Even when we control that anger, it feels so powerful that we worry about what we might do if we "lost it." Sometimes we do . . . . and what follows, of course, are feelings of guilt.

Telling someone not to feel guilty is futile. Besides, guilty feelings can be quite useful if they lead us to rethink some of the situations that brought those feelings about. For example, recently I wrote about a mom who was upset and worried because her child refused to leave school with her when she came to pick him up. In fact, she was really quite angry with him for not appreciating the effort involved for her in leaving work to come to school. As a working mom, her son's behavior felt to her like a reproach for being away from him.

In fact, it may very well have been a reproach on her son's part, but that didn't mean she was doing a bad thing by working. Children don't like everything we do. They don't have to. Underneath it all was *her own* unresolved conflict about working—her feelings of guilt about not being there full time. And it was these feelings that got in the way of her ability to simply acknowledge her son's feelings.

I have seen many instances in which a mother's conflict about working leads her to go over and beyond anything realistic in what she does to make up for her own guilt. Invariably this kind of sacrifice leads to anger, which, if expressed, leads to more guilt. So that when we say that a child pushes our buttons, we are usually referring to something unresolved within ourselves that makes us over-react. This doesn't mean that a child's behavior may not be provocative, even unacceptable. What it does mean is that if we are reacting to something within ourselves, that becomes a handicap in responding to our child's behavior effectively. Our own anger and then the guilt it causes get in our way.

Another mom talked about how guilty she feels for blowing up when her daughter comes out of her room after being put to bed at night. As a working mom, she spends every minute she can with her child when she gets home; but by the end of the evening she has nothing left to give. Dad has offered to do the bedtime; but mom won't let him because of her feeling that somehow she has to make up for all the time she *is* away. Here, too, it is her own conflict about working that leads her to compensate inappropriately, with an outcome that only makes her feel worse.

Mothers who are home with their children can also get caught up in the same kind of feelings. A mom wrote to me about the anger and frustration she feels when after a whole day of doing things for and with her children, they complain about something she hasn't done. She finds herself trying to prove to them how much she *has* done for them. It seems that many mothers today have a completely unrealistic idea about what they should be doing to qualify as "good mothers', and end up paying for these ideas with anger and guilt.

Sometimes, it is when children behave in ways that were not tolerated when mom herself was a child that leads mothers to blow up and then feel guilty. Mom was made to feel like a "bad girl" when she did those things, and now she feels like a "bad mother" when her children do them. Her reaction is out of proportion to the behavior, because it has touched off something within herself.

The point is not to use guilt feelings to beat yourself up about something you think you did that you regret. Use them constructively to take a step back and rethink what happened. In the same way that understanding your children's behavior can help you become more effective in dealing with them, understanding your own behavior can accomplish the same thing. Ask yourself what it really was that was bothering you. If you can get in touch with those feelings instead of the guilt, it can help you figure out a better ending the next time around.

Nobody's Perfect

That title is the famous last line from the movie "Some Like It Hot". The response the Jack Lemmon character gets when he admits that he is a man—after having pretended to be a woman—is, "Nobody's perfect!"

I thought of that line recently when a mother who reads my blog told me that she doesn't like the title—Good Enough Mothering. She said she doesn't want to be "good enough", she wants to be perfect. "Good enough" doesn't seem good enough. She told me that when her first child was born she knew nothing about children and read everything she could so she wouldn't make any mistakes.

To my surprise, a day or two later, another mother said almost the same thing. Although she said it somewhat tongue-in-cheek, she admitted that she wants to be perfect. She talked about it in connection with the stress of mothering—the attempt to be perfect.

It was not surprising to me to find that mothers are trying to be perfect. My purpose in writing this blog is to try to help mothers give that up. What was surprising was to hear this stated as if it were an attainable goal. Two questions that occurred to me are, what is the definition of perfect, and how would you know if you had achieved it?

Would being a perfect mother mean having children who are perfect? That sounds like an impossible goal on the face of it. But if that is the test it would mean that any fault in your child would mean that you did something wrong—that you aren't perfect. So is that part of the demand for perfection that mothers sometimes have for their children?

Does being perfect mean not making any mistakes? One of the moms I refer to said she didn't want to make any mistakes. What is a mistake? And how would you know if you made one? If your child is unhappy, or frustrated, or angry, does that mean you made a mistake? It would seem this judgment depends on children's behavior. What your children do defines you as a mother—as if children's behavior is a result only of what you did or didn't do.

Does being perfect mean fitting some image you have of what a mother is supposed to be like? Someone like your mother, or the opposite of your mother, or the mother you wished you had? Everyone experiences frustration while growing up because living in the world with other people inevitably brings some frustration. Mothers almost always are blamed as the source of that frustration. Would being perfect mean your children would never blame you for anything? If that is the case, to be perfect you would have to be an all-gratifying mother, let your children eat whatever they want, do whatever they want, get whatever they want. How would that work out?

The idea of being a perfect mother seems to suggest that your children are like lumps of clay that you can mold—they are your product, your creation. If you do everything the right way you can make that creation into anything you want. This leaves out not only all the inborn factors that make each child a specific individual, but also all the other influences that come to bear during a child's development.

If being a perfect mother means having your child turn out a certain way—the way you want—what is that way you want him or her to turn out? What measuring rod will you use to determine if you are, or have been, a perfect mother? Mothers often ask what the right way is to do this or that. But the right way for what? For the child to be happy, never to find anything hard, never to be disappointed, never to feel upset? To be successful? If so, what is your definition of success? An A average in school, a great athlete, the most popular in the class, someone who cares about others?

It seems clear that what it comes down to is essentially a matter of values. What is it that you as parents value most? Is it academic success, success in sports, making money, being creative, contributing to society? The answers to these questions are going to vary from parent to parent because people differ and what they value differs. And your own values are the determining factor in how you raise your children.

The idea that there is some abstract right way of doing things simply doesn't work. The way you respond to your child depends on who you are, who your child is, and what you value most. This determines what you are trying to accomplish and how you try to accomplish it.

At the end of the day, as a parent it is who you are that matters—not whether you do it the "right way". Nobody's perfect!

Is This Normal?

When mothers ask me about a child's behavior that worries them, or that they have some concern about, the question that almost always comes up is whether the behavior is "normal". What they are really asking is whether the behavior is "abnormal", meaning, "Does this mean there is something wrong with my child?"

A mother recently asked me this question about her child who would not talk to his baby sitter after having been told that she would be leaving. Another mom asked this about her son refusing to leave school with her when she picked him up, although he had cried when she left him in the morning. The question often comes up when a child's behavior doesn't fit a mother's picture of what is appropriate, or creates a problem for mom.

What does "normal" really mean? Sometimes mothers mean, "Is this typical of all children?" Another meaning can be, "Is it natural for a child to do this?" The implication is that if it is "typical", or "natural", the behavior is o.k. If it is not, then something is wrong with the behavior and possibly with the child who is behaving this way. The behavior then becomes a symptom of a deeper "problem".

But is this really true? In fact, normal does not mean good or bad. It means in the nature of things. It may be in the nature of a young child to want his own way, to get angry about things expected of him, even to have a tantrum when frustrated. But that doesn't mean the behavior is acceptable, or is not something the child may need help mastering.

Too often mothers think that if difficult behavior is normal there is nothing they can, or should do about it. The problem is that children express their feelings and wishes in behavior, and some behavior can be provocative and makes parents angry. Many times we react to such behavior with an urge to punish children in an attempt to stop the behavior. But the idea that the behavior is normal seems to lead to the feeling that maybe parents are supposed to just accept the behavior they don't like.

Mothers, at times, feel guilty if they punish behavior that is "normal". This is where the worry about "doing the wrong thing" comes into play. They are afraid that punishment, or their own anger, might damage their children in some way. Mothers have often expressed to me the fear that some day a child would be talking "on the couch" about something she did to him in anger. These feelings can lead a mother to the conclusion that there is nothing she *can* do.

But the fact is, behavior that upsets parents is also behavior that can tell us what our children are trying to say to us. For young children, behavior is their primary means of communicating their feelings. Even when we don't like the behavior, understanding what a child is saying is the path to knowing what to do about it. Hopefully, we will eventually be able to help him tell us about it in a better way. But first we have to understand what it means.

Understanding behavior does not mean there is no need or no way to respond to it. Part of our responsibility as parents is to teach our children that some behavior is not acceptable. (More later about ways to do that.) But the first point is that thinking about whether behavior is normal or not is not helpful. The child who is refusing to look at his baby sitter is simply expressing his anger at her for leaving. The child who refuses to leave school with his mom may be telling her that since she left him, he is now leaving her. In understanding that, the first mom will be less worried about the behavior and able to sympathize with her child about his feeling of anger at the loss. For the second mom, understanding her son's behavior may lessen her feeling of rejection—and perhaps, also, any feeling of anger about being rejected. Letting children know that you understand their feelings, even if you don't like their behavior, is often a first step in helping them change.

No Fault Mothering

Not everything children do is caused by something you did. That seems obvious doesn't it? Yet what seems sensible often has nothing to do with the way mothers feel. The idea that there is a right and a wrong way to do everything is so much part of parents' thinking, that when a child's behavior is worrisome mothers often come to the conclusion that *they* must have done something wrong.

Working mothers are quick to attribute behavior they are concerned about to the fact that they are working. One mother talked to me about her daughter who had suddenly started stuttering. Mom was sure it was due to a business trip that had taken her away from home for several days. She seemed to feel that she had to defend herself for continuing to work outside the home.

Stuttering can come and go in young children, so Mom and I talked about what else was going on in her daughter's life. It became clear that the little girl was feeling a lot of pressure about toilet training, which was also going on. The follow-up was that they relaxed about the toilet training and the stuttering disappeared. Maybe it would have stopped anyway, who knows? But the point is that Mom was so quick to blame herself for working that she wasn't thinking about anything else.

Another mother, who had stopped working to stay home with her child, told me that the transition from work to child-rearing was very challenging. She said the most difficult thing was the feeling of ultimate responsibility—that no matter what else she was doing, she always was responsible for her child.

Another difficult thing was never knowing if she was doing a good job—always worrying after she had done something if she had done it the "right" way. It was not like work where people told you whether you had done it right, and you could feel confident.

This Mom expressed very well the feelings I have heard from many mothers, both those at-home and those working outside the home. Young children are dependent on us for their care, and that feeling of ultimate responsibility can lead mothers to feel that everything is due to them—both bad and good. (Unfortunately, they get blamed for the bad, and get little credit for the good.)

And it certainly is true that as mothers we don't get any positive feedback in the form of a promotion, or a raise. You don't know how your children are going to turn out, and you're in trouble if you look to their behavior to tell you how *you* are doing. Children are not going to like some of the things we do as parents because we *are* responsible for them, and they often show it in behavior that is difficult, or that we don't like.

In the same way, thinking in terms of whether children are happy or unhappy can lead you down the garden path. Is anyone happy all the time? Yet mothers often think that when children seem unhappy it means they (the mothers) did something wrong to cause it. The fact is that parents and children live in two different realities: what parents require is often not at all what children want, and what children want is often not possible or realistic. So children express their unhappiness at this state of affairs, which is what we all do at times. But this should not be translated as meaning we did something wrong.

The point is that blaming yourself for everything a child does is not helpful for several reasons. For one thing, it makes mothers feel unnecessarily guilty and worried, which makes life more difficult. But perhaps more importantly, it interferes with the ability to do something constructive about the situation at hand. If you start out with the idea that you have done something wrong, you get focused on yourself rather than on your child. You get so involved in thinking about what you did to cause something, that you forget to think about what else might be going on for your child.

We forget that growing up is just not that easy for anyone, and often think that if only our own parents had done this or that differently, our own growing up would have been easier. So we sometimes get caught up in the goal of doing it the "right way" for our own children. But the fact is that our children's behavior is often a reflection of their own struggle to deal with the changes taking place within themselves as they grow, as well as meeting the changing expectations of those around them.

As with the mother of the stuttering little girl, if you stop trying to figure out what *you* did to cause something, and think instead about what else might be going on for your child, you will be taking a step toward helping the situation. Not every problem has a solution, and there is no "right" answer or thing to do. We can only do our best to try to understand what *is* going on, and in that way let our children know that whatever they are going through, we are there to help them.

DEVELOPMENTAL STEPS

Expectations

A mother wrote to me saying that the problem she thinks she is having with her children is that she never knows where to set her expectations. That is such an important issue because in a way it goes to the heart of child-rearing. The question really is, does what we expect from a child match where he or she is developmentally and what he or she is capable of doing? Often when we seem to have hit a snag, that's where the problem lies.

The question we're trying to answer is not as simple as it may seem. Sometimes mothers try to answer it by looking at charts that tell you what children are supposed to be doing at different ages. Sometimes we compare our own children to others of the same age. This is not very helpful because not only is every child different, but one's own child is a real child, not the hypothetical child of the charts.

Also, the question is challenging because there are different aspects to development: physical, intellectual, emotional, social, and a range of development within each one. Children's development often varies from one area to another. These various areas of development don't all grow and develop evenly, or at the same pace. This can be confusing in terms of what we expect, since next steps in some things may not relate to where a child is in others.

For example, what we often find is a child jumping ahead with many skills, such as learning letters or numbers, playing complicated games, having interesting conversations. Yet that same child may resist dressing herself, or start to act babyish, or continue to provoke a younger sibling. Also, children's understanding of what we are asking of them is usually way ahead of their doing what we ask. That's why when you ask him over and over again to "stop doing that", it often does no good, even though he understands what you are asking.

Our children may show their ability to reason and yet seem unreasonable in their behavior. Aside from the fact that what seems reasonable to them may not seem reasonable to us, there are other factors that influence their behavior. One big one is impulse control. A child's ability to control the expression of his feeling in behavior—not to strike out when angry, or to throw something when frustrated—often lags behind his understanding that he is not supposed to do that. Understanding and control are two different skills which may not be in synch with each other.

Another major influence on children's behavior is their ongoing conflict about dependence and independence. The push for autonomy is very strong and can lead children to try to assert themselves in ways that run counter to what we want them to do at any particular time. At the same time, independence can feel a little scary for a child himself. You still need and want to be taken care of by mom and dad. Maybe you'll lose that if you act too grown up. The struggle between the wish both to be independent and dependent can account for the puzzling babyish behavior that pops up from time to time in a child who otherwise seems so mature.

So, how can we tell what is appropriate to expect of our children at any given point? Part of the problem may be with the word "expect" itself. It suggests that a child is supposed to do something and that it is bad behavior or something else is wrong if he doesn't do it. Most often when we think a child is capable of behaving in a certain way, or doing something we ask, we expect him to do it.

As we've seen, the ability to do something is made up of a number of different skills. When we seem to be getting stuck on something we think a child should be able to do, it is helpful to think first about whether our expectation matches what we know about our own particular child. What part of what we are expecting may be hard for her? If she becomes clingy in new situations, do we also know that she is a child who is slow to warm up? If he persists in annoying his little brother, is he resisting the message we have been giving that he is supposed to be the grown-up big brother?

Parents are both leaders and followers. We follow the leads children give us through their behavior, but we also lead them to the next step.

In general, a good rule of thumb is to be slightly ahead of where a child is—not where we think he should be—while at the same time leading by showing the way to where we want him to go. When a child is having difficulty, we may have to take a step back in order to help him take a step forward. But we always have to keep in mind where we are going so that we ourselves don't get stuck in the step back.

Fidgeters

Recently, I found myself smiling while having a conversation with my teen-age grandson. "You are a fidgeter", I told him. He asked me what that meant and I explained that it meant fiddling in an absent minded way with anything at hand. He was startled, not having realized that was what he was doing. He also seemed reassured when I told him that all the boys in our family were fidgeters. That in fact, many boys are fidgeters. Sometimes girls are, too. But more often, it's the boys.

What brought a smile to my face during this conversation was the memory of my children doing exactly the same thing when they were growing up. My grandson smiled, too, when I told him how his father always fidgeted with the cord on the window blind, for he seemed to feel he was in good company.

Of course, I can't say I was smiling at the time. Actually, I know it drove me crazy and I'm sure I was a real pest, constantly saying, "STOP FIDGETING." But one thing I know that is different between then and now is that it never occurred to me that the fidgeting was a sign of anything other than the restless energy of a growing boy. Mothers today are not that fortunate, because the world around them has created anxiety about all sorts of behavior. What used to be just the description of a child now often is seen as a symptom—and something to worry about.

We have an ideal in our culture of valuing the individual. Yet, in reality, there is little tolerance of individual differences in development and in personality. Increasingly the emphasis is on norms—the achievement of skills and behavior at specified times in development. Somehow the idea of a developmental spectrum within the norms has gotten lost; the fact that individual children are at different points on that spectrum.

The pressure on children—and on their parents—to meet set expectations has come from several sources. Often it comes from schools, where overcrowding and other difficulties result in large classes and little opportunity to meet individual needs. It is easier to manage a class where children are compliant. Unfortunately, it also becomes easier to label a child a "problem" than first to try to understand what that "problem" is coming from.

Sometimes parents who themselves have many pressures may also set unrealistic expectations for their children. If you have been working all day, have to make dinner, clean up and do other chores, it is hard to find the time and energy to understand and deal with behavior that is asking for attention. But parents want to do what is best for their children and are quick to worry if there are suggestions that evaluations or special help is needed.

The fact that evaluations and interventions for young children are available is, of course, all to the good. But there is also a downside. Too often behavior that is simply a more intense expression of things children are experiencing or feeling becomes suspect. Good examples are children with high activity levels or strong emotional reactions. There is a wide range of behavior in these areas in young children. Not every active child is hyperactive, or has an attention deficit disorder. Not every child who is sensitive, or who cries easily, has a mood disorder.

What has happened is that behavior has too often become pathologized—looked upon as symptomatic of a disorder, and too quickly labeled as such. In general, we all have a need to give something a name. It's as though naming it (which is what a label does) tells us what it is and what to do about it. It somehow makes everyone feel better, as though the problem—now identified—is now solved. This may be true if it is the measles, but not so true when it comes to developmental issues in childhood.

Yes, real developmental problems do exist, and we certainly want the interventions that can help. But often it is not that clear what the problem is and what will help most. The result, at times, is a "more is better" philosophy. Children may then be overloaded with therapies which in turn put more pressure on them and their parents, and tend to overlook or ignore their more general needs as growing children.

The point is that too quickly labeling behavior—and looking at it in terms of a diagnosis—can prevent us as parents or teachers from first trying to understand behavior as something a child is telling us about himself. What is he saying about himself and his life experience? Are our expectations in synch with his abilities? Are some behaviors consistent with his overall personality? Is something going on too stressful for him? Is this developmental stage more bumpy for him than others?

As parents we know our children best. We need to think through our own answers before accepting too readily the opinions of friends, family—or even teachers. Mothers should trust themselves. You know more than you think you do.

Starting School

Many of you have young children who are just starting nursery school—or even a pre-nursery group. A mom called me recently worrying in advance about "separation anxiety". She was concerned, as many mothers seem to be, that her child would be upset when it was time to separate, and would not "let her leave". Other mothers who have already found this happening, question if this means there is a "problem". "Separation anxiety" seems to be one of those bugaboos that have become heavy with meaning.

Why does this loom so large in mothers' minds? On a practical level, many of you are working and look forward to your child being productively engaged while you are as well. Beyond that, separation is a step toward independence—your child is growing up. The beginning of more freedom for mom! But that can be experienced as a double-edged sword. Another cut in the umbilical cord. Sometimes it's hard to let go of those baby years when everything is mommy, mommy, mommy.

Children may feel two ways about growing up—just as we do. So there are concerns on both sides about next steps. Mother and child are both not quite sure if they can make it. There are challenges here for both. Children are just beginning to develop the skills they need to get along successfully with others. They are learning to share, take turns, control their impulses and "use their words", among other things. They may be a little concerned about their ability to do all this without mom or a familiar adult there to help.

Mothers are often concerned about the same thing. You worry about whether your children will "measure up". Will they meet expectations, behave in ways that you (or others) think they should? And if they don't, is that a reflection on you as a mother? Or does it mean that your children are not developing as they should? These feelings on both sides get expressed one way or another in the separation process, sometimes in children's tears of protest, or in a mother's uncertainty about letting go.

The trouble is that this normal developmental step has been mystified as "separation anxiety". The name itself makes it seem as if something is terribly wrong—as though if a child doesn't just happily say goodby at the door he is not well adjusted. As if separation is a test of your ability as a mother: if your child is finding it hard, that means you did something wrong. If there is no upset, it means you are a success.

In reality, the term "separation anxiety" is a description of a usual developmental step in which children become increasingly aware of being a separate person from mom. Why anxiety? Because being attached to mom has both benefits and drawbacks. On the one hand your needs are met and you are taken care of. But on the other hand, you may want to do things that mom doesn't want you to do and might make her angry. The conflict about being dependent or independent often continues throughout life. But for little children it is a new experience and may cause anxiety.

Some children may feel more anxiety than others, or at different points in their development than others. Not everyone is in the same place at the same time just because adults have decided to put children in "separation groups" at ever earlier ages. The question is: if this is a developmental bump for your own child, how can you best help him or her over it?

Perhaps most useful is the recognition that your child's tears or protests when you leave do not mean that something bad is happening. The fact that your child cries does not mean you are doing a bad thing—even though a child's cry may feel accusatory. She is saying something about herself—not about you. What she may be saying is that she needs some reassurance, not just that you'll be back for her, but that she is going to be o.k. without you. Children are often further upset by their own emotions, so it helps them to know that it's all right if they miss mom and that they will feel better soon. If you are upset, it confirms to your child that there is something to be upset about. If you are not worried, that helps her not worry. Your acceptance and reassurance makes the situation feel less threatening.

Of course, there are times when a child's upset is telling you that the separation is really too hard at this particular time in her development. It can be challenging for a parent to determine whether or not a child can master these feelings or if a familiar person needs to continue to be there. What can help is learning how well your child is able to regroup after you leave.

We all gain strength from finding we can master difficult situations, and the same is true for our children. So even when your child is upset, finding that he can overcome those feelings will help him grow. Sometimes when you hear that your child has settled down after you leave, it can feel like manipulation—"he was just doing that to get me to stay". Yes, your child may be trying to get you to stay, but that doesn't mean that his feelings aren't genuine, that he isn't really worried about your leaving.

It's important to remember that this is a process which may take more—or less—time. Building a relationship with a new person—in this case the teacher—is what helps children accept the separation from parent or caregiver. As the parent, you (with the help of the teacher) can make the judgment about where your own child is. Many of you who are working or have other time pressures, may not be able to give as much time as you would like to this process. And this is a reality of life which children can learn to live with. This learning may take longer than we would like, but here, too, can be helped along by understanding and accepting our children's feelings—as well as our own.

User Friendly Limits

A mom I know asked me a question about setting limits. I wasn't surprised, because her son is two years old. That's just about the time children start to show that they have a mind of their own and want to use it. They can become quite self-assertive about what they want and don't want to do. Mothers are bewildered by the transformation in their formerly easy-to-manage, cuddly babies.

This transformation becomes what has often been called the "terrible twos". What makes them seem terrible is the potential for confrontation in children's changed behavior around this time. It is a potential for confrontation that continues through much of a child's development—becoming particularly difficult once again in adolescence. Questions about setting limits can go on for quite a while!

But I think two year olds get a bad rap. While their behavior can seem challenging, once you're on to them they can be quite interesting—and fun. There are so many exciting things going on in their development. It's exactly those developmental changes that are part of the new self-assertion. New motor skills enable children at this stage to run, climb and jump, among other things. Climbing means pulling a chair over to the cabinet to reach the high shelf where mom keeps the cookies. The ability to figure things out and develop strategies is also an unfolding skill. Most significant, children are increasingly able to use language, and "no" is an early favorite word of choice. It is the big "no" that opens the road to confrontation with parents.

That "no" is actually part of another change that otherwise is less visible. Children are becoming more aware now that they and mom are separate people. What they want is not always what mom wants, and what mom wants them to do is not always what they want to do. The conflict caused by this increasing awareness can be very confusing. Children want what they want, but they also want and need mom's care and approval.

A child's inner confusion gets expressed in behavior that is then confusing to mom. He loves the bath but suddenly is refusing to take a bath. Mom cuts the peanut butter and jelly sandwich in quarters as she always does, and a melt-down follows because he wants the sandwich whole. Nothing will do but to make that sandwich whole again. No wonder mothers tear their hair in frustration.

What makes this behavior challenging is that there is not one clear way for a mother to respond that "works". Obviously that particular sandwich can't be made whole again as the child demands. One can only sympathize and wait for the upset to subside. But there are other situations where a mother will do best by just moving ahead with what she has in mind—despite the child's protests. Children don't have to like something, or want to do it, in order to do it. (One mother I knew thought she had to persuade her child that he loved the bath in order to get him to take one.)

The real frustration for a mother comes after she has been reasonable and offered to make another sandwich, or give the child another five minutes to play, and then still has to deal with the protest or tantrum. This is what leads to the "do it, or else" approach that often leads to confrontation big time. On the other hand, it also can lead to a mother just giving up and doing whatever a child wants. No happy solution either way.

This is what led to the mom's question about setting limits. She was aware that she willingly kept reading more and more books at bedtime, but then when he wanted to play rather than eat lunch, she wasn't sure if she shouldn't just pick him up screaming and bring him to the table. Her impulse was to do whatever he wanted to make him (and herself) happy, but that was leading to a forceful approach at other times. So, how to "set limits"?

That phrase has a somewhat threatening sound—SET LIMITS—as if a guard rail or some kind of barrier is suddenly about to drop. OFF LIMITS—GO NO FURTHER. Sometimes it means a parent has reached her limit in tolerating certain behavior. That can happen if you go too far down the child's road, and then as a result have to come to an abrupt stop.

Actually, limits can be more effective as part of a process in which we *help* children move on, rather than demanding that they do so. Basically that means recognizing that not only when they are two, but for a while to come, we are asking them to do many things that run counter to what they want and feel. Even when setting limits, we need to show respect for those wishes and feelings. It is the same kind of respect we would like to be shown when we are asked to do something we may not be ready to do.

Limits can be made user friendly. That means being clear about expectations while allowing our children time to meet them. We don't have to become "the enemy"—even when asking children to give up their wishes for ours. It takes time to learn that "you can't always have what you want"—both for parents and children.

The Expert Dawdlers

Probably the two complaints about children I hear most from mothers have to do with getting out in the morning and going to bed at night. In the morning there is always that rush, rush to get going. At night, after who knows how many books read and whatever else, mothers are really ready to say goodnight.

But children are not that eager to get ready to leave their home or go to their bed. We can all identify with such feelings—it would be so nice just to hang out at home in the morning. Unfortunately, as grown-ups we do what we have to do. We're not as expert at dawdling as our children.

Actually, these two parts of the day—beginnings and endings—have something in common. Both involve transitions, which are always difficult for young children. Morning means leaving home for the outside world. So much nicer to stay in your pajamas and play. Night is even harder, having to leave play for bed, having to leave wakefulness for sleep.

Something else these two transitions have in common is that they are both separations: leaving home and parents in the morning, leaving parents—and whatever they are still doing—at night. Even as adults, there are situations that evoke for us feelings about separation. Some people call that the Sunday night blues. For children, who are still very much engaged in dealing with separation, these feelings surface readily. So these two difficult times of day mean transitions and separations. No wonder they're hard.

At a recent workshop with parents, this topic came up for discussion. One mom told us something interesting about her four year old. When he first learned to dress himself he was proud as could be, and would rush to get dressed in the morning without even being told. Now that he has mastered it, however, he is completely disinterested, dawdles, and finds any excuse not to get dressed. Mom has tried many ways to deal with this to no avail.

In our discussion, I asked if her son ever asks her to dress him, and she said he does. This is interesting, because it tells us something important about a process children go through. They love to master new skills and feel very good about themselves when they succeed. On the other hand, there is a downside. Every step toward independence means a step away from dependence on—or help from—mom. Children are not altogether sure they are ready to give that up. The road to independence is not a straight line forward. It zig-zags back and forth a bit when taking next steps.

The problem, however, is that as mothers we are delighted when children master new things and are capable of doing more for themselves. But once children show us they are capable of doing something, we begin to expect it and can feel resentful when suddenly they resist doing what we know they now can do on their own. What we once did for them happily, can now feel like a burden and become a source of conflict. A child may feel this resistance from mom and meet it with resistance of his own.

This is one of those situations where we really can meet children part way. We can say, "Let me help you get started", without going down that slippery slope of just dressing him, which sometimes feels as though it would be easier. But it's not, in the end. Children, at times, may be all too happy to slip back into being taken care of—at least in this area. So help needn't mean to "do for". But your *willingness* to help can go a long way in overcoming his resistance—and can also reassure him that his own growing capabilities don't mean losing Mom.

Another approach that can be helpful is something I call changing the subject. When your child starts protesting when you try to hurry him along, instead of getting into a back and forth of "you have to", "I don't want to", start talking about something else, such as which friend will get to school first today, or what you will be doing together after school or tonight. Usually, if you keep up the "hurry, hurry" commentary, children just tune you out.

Mostly, the difficulty we have with children and routines, is an expression of their resistance to being pulled into meeting the demands of the adult world. They want to be in that world—but on their own terms. It's something we all struggle with as parents, but to the extent that we can lead them, rather than pull them, we're that much ahead of the game. The suggestions here may help, but I have found in my work with parents that once you understand your child's behavior, you yourselves come up with the best solutions.

More About Transitions

A mother told me about overhearing her daughter and friends playing with their dolls. She was stunned to suddenly hear, "Hurry, hurry. Have to hurry up now. You can't go, if you're not ready." It was her daughter speaking but she was hearing herself. It always comes as a shock to discover how we sound to our children.

Often what is jarring in the playback we get from our children is the bossy tone. When you hear them correcting or instructing their pretend children, the authoritative and critical voice is greatly exaggerated—at least we hope it's an exaggeration. But what it tells us is that even if we don't sound quite like that, it *feels* like that to them. One of the conditions of childhood is that you get told what to do a lot. And since children don't do what they are asked or told to do as quickly as we would like them to, the scolding voice probably surfaces more than we imagine.

Our attempts to move children along during transitions often seem to provoke a rebellious response. They are either openly defiant or seem not to have heard us. They are engaged in what they are doing—even when it seems as though they are doing nothing—and are determined to move at their own pace, not ours. They don't like our insistence on our schedule, not theirs.

If you want to identify with your child's feelings and behavior, imagine the following scenario: you and your spouse are going out, and after first having to do a number of chores you are trying to finish combing your hair, or putting on makeup. Then you hear from your mate, "What, you're not ready? We have to leave right now or we're going to be late." Instead of being able to finish in your own way, someone is standing over you, telling you with great annoyance to hurry up.

Did you ever find yourself saying, "Don't treat me like a child!"? That seems to be saying, "I'm an adult—don't boss me around the way you would a child". Does that mean we think children have to be treated that way? Actually, children would like to be treated the way we would like to be treated. When children are angry about being told what to do, a familiar battle cry of theirs is, "You're not the boss over me!"

Of course, we are responsible for our children. That means we are trying to teach them how to live in the world—a world that has schedules, chores to be done, and often the need to comply with others' requests that we may not like. One difference between us and our children is that we, hopefully, have learned those lessons. Also, growth and maturation have given us the ability to carry them out.

Young children do not yet have the skills needed to switch focus, to move readily from one thing to the next. They don't yet have our sense of time or the ability to be future oriented. They are not thinking ahead about the next thing on the agenda, even if it is something that we know they would like. And they definitely are not yet multitaskers!

Leaving play to have lunch or take a bath feels like a real intrusion. It is not only that what we are asking them to do next doesn't seem relevant. It is also the frustration at having to leave something that is pleasurable. One of the difficult tasks of childhood is mastering the ability to tolerate such frustration.

So what seems like a simple matter of following routines really presents a number of difficulties: making transitions is in itself hard for children, and the frustration this involves is something they still haven't mastered. Then at the point in development at which their wish for autonomy comes into it, they begin to rebel against being told what to do—being "bossed".

Once we recognize what some of the factors are that lead to our own frustration with children and routines, it becomes easier to see what we might do to ease the pain. Most basic, is to accept that children really do need help as they are learning to master following the routines that we take for granted. That means literally helping them move from one thing to the next. Giving repeated verbal commands with escalating annoyance is not going to do it.

The most obvious kind of help is giving lead time whenever possible. "Soon it will be time to leave" or "Time for one more game before dinner." Giving those signals at several intervals before you "really mean it" can help. Most nursery schools use signals of one kind or another such as switching the light off and on, to alert children to the fact that it is time for the next thing.

But very often what is most helpful is actually being there to help your child move along; to help her start getting dressed or to help him start putting toys away. Your presence becomes the bridge that enables your child to shift gears. We sometimes resent doing that, feeling that children "should" be able to do what we ask just because we've asked them. That may be the goal, but words by themselves may not get us—or them—there.

"Poop" Talk

There is a wonderful book called "Everyone Poops", that many moms have found helpful when toilet training their children. It's true that everyone poops, and it is also true that many children go through a "poop talk" phase during which bathroom language suddenly makes an appearance, much to the chagrin of parents. Usually, children are in pre-school programs around this time and distraught mothers often attribute the use of such language to other children in school.

While children's horizons do broaden once they are out in a larger social world, and the "poop talk" is not just a product of spontaneous combustion, children at this stage do share a common interest in body functions. The process of toilet training puts the focus on one's body and what comes out of it. Young children have a great interest in their own poop—by whatever name it has been designated in their own family.

Many children do not start out sharing the sounds and facial expressions conveying "dirty" or "disgusting" that adults express. The poop comes out of their bodies and as such has value. Often, children are reluctant to part with it and resist the toilet where it is flushed away and disappears. It is as though they have lost part of their bodies. Sometimes children may be reluctant to take that next step to more independent functioning that parting with diapers implies.

Toilet training itself involves mastering the control needed to meet adult requirements that these functions be regulated according to time and place. Children are working hard—at times under adult pressure—to establish such control. What better outlet than to substitute words for the actual poop. Instead of the poop coming out of your body, the words can come out of your mouth without control. Unhappily, the words seem just as unacceptable to mom and dad as does the poop in the pull-ups.

Trying to get children to control their words at the same time that they are trying to control the poop itself, is something of a lost cause. Or more to the point, trying to stop children from talking poop is futile. If you think about it, we end up trying to control two things at once, body function and speech. And this at a point in development where children are apt to be somewhat defiant about controls anyway.

What most parents learn—often the hard way—is that once children find they can get a rise out of you, they are delighted to do it again, and again. At first it can seem like a bit of teasing. But if parents become more punitive or threatening in their responses, children are apt to become more defiant, and no-win confrontations are the result. Your children have discovered that some words have a lot of power!

At some point interest in poop and bathroom talk fades out. But the interest in the body does not, and poop words often mutate into genital words. This may coincide with a time when there is greater awareness and interest in the differences between boys' and girls' bodies. Without getting too Freudian with thoughts of castration anxiety, just paying attention to the behavior of little boys is enough to persuade you that they seek to reassure themselves that their male equipment is intact. Here, too, the use of words contributes to a sense of mastery and power. Little boys enjoy affirming their maleness—particularly with their mothers—by the assertive way they repeat names for genitals. The shock value alone can give them a sense of power.

So how can we respond to "poop talk" and the later stages of provocative talk and name calling that follow? The talk seems to serve a useful purpose in helping children master other concerns they may have about their bodies and body functions. But the other side of this is that they also function in a social world where certain language is considered inappropriate. (Although sometimes it is hard to tell if there are any boundaries left anymore.)

Actually, the spontaneous reaction of parents when such language first appears makes it immediately clear to children that their parents disapprove. Only when it is turned into a big issue do children use it to bait their parents, and ongoing conflict is created. You can let children know that you recognize how much they enjoy saying these words but that other people don't enjoy hearing them. After that, the most useful policy is to ignore the language and change the subject. Without the reaction, the provocation loses its appeal.

With "poop talk" and its later variants, children sometimes are expressing confusion or asking a question about something they or others are experiencing. You may be able to recognize that in the context of their talk, or in the way they are using the language. If children sound mixed up or confused in what they are saying, it can be helpful to let them know that, and to ask if there is something they would like to ask or to know more about.

But most of the time talking poop is just what kids do—just like they poop.

Playing By The Rules

Have you played a game of Candyland, or some modern version of Go Fish with your preschooler and noticed how rarely it resembles the instructions on the box? If you ask your child how to play this game you may get a rough outline of what the idea is, but more often what you're told is where to start and where to finish.

"It doesn't matter if you win or lose, it's how you play the game". Nonsense! It doesn't matter how you play the game, the point is to win. Young children have little interest in rules—although they may pay lip service to the idea in order to placate parents. They improvise as they go along, moving their pieces in whatever direction serves their purpose. And the purpose is to be the winner!

If you try to correct your child and tell her the rules don't permit the way she is playing, she may argue with you and want to prove that those moves are allowed. Or else she may tell you that this game is being played by different rules and she is allowed to do what she is doing. If you persist in your corrections you may find your child telling you that the game is boring, or she really doesn't want to play this game anymore.

Parents often take a dim view of this behavior. If a child takes more turns than allowed, or jumps ahead of where he is supposed to be, they may tell him he is cheating, or otherwise express disapproval. Sometimes a game that was supposed to be fun ends up badly because mom or dad and their child have different points of view. The child's interest is in winning, mom and dad are interested in how he plays the game.

Most parents are aware of their child's intense wish to win, but it makes them a little uncomfortable. It's as if there is something "not nice" about showing this unabashed need to win. As if it is a moral failing, or a character flaw. Mothers often ask me if it is "right", purposely to let children win. They are worried if a child expects, or wants to win all the time, and report conflicts with peers over this.

Wouldn't we all like to win? What is it about children being so up front about it that bothers us? The problem is we're making adult judgments about children's behavior. We have all had to learn how to express the wish to win in socially acceptable ways—for some of us it is harder than others. Children's open and at times aggressive behavior in expressing this wish often comes too close to the feelings we ourselves have had to shut down or modify. We worry that our children aren't doing that.

Winning is more fun than losing, and very young children are still operating under the pleasure principle. Growing up involves deferring immediate pleasure to achieve longer range goals. The tools needed to accomplish this are acquired as part of development. In particular, intelligence and evolving thought processes enable the ability to reason, and to make meaningful action possible. You can figure out strategies to win!

If you watch six or seven year olds playing a game, you will find them spending more time discussing and arguing about the rules than in playing the game. The rules now have become very important—even though they may be changed with every play. This is also the stage when children may be quick to report someone else who is not following the rules—a sign that they are still struggling within themselves about obeying rules.

These developmental changes take place as part of a greater interest in peers and new patterns of socialization. It is appropriate that rules begin to loom larger at this time, because rules are a necessary part of social interaction. We need rules not just to play games, but to cross the street without risking being hit by a car, to wait our turn when there is a line, and not to take property that doesn't belong to us, among other things.

So, of course it is part of our job as parents to teach children about rules. The question, as always, is how we do that. When we tell a young child in a judgmental way that he is cheating, we are imposing an adult concept that he is not yet able to fully understand or use appropriately.

What he gets from that is that he has done something bad without really understanding why the grownups think it is wrong. The rule has gotten separated from its reason for being.

If instead we acknowledge that it is fun to win and that other people like to win, too, there is a better basis for helping a child understand that playing the game may mean losing as well as winning. Rules are there to give everyone a fair chance. But as parents, we need to remember that accepting that is a process that takes time and experience.

If we are more accepting of our children's wish to win, they may in the end be better able to accept losing.

Apologies

Mothers often ask me about altercations between children, either at home on play dates, or in the park. The usual event is that one child strikes out in some way, either physically or verbally, because the other child has taken something he was playing with, or because the other child won't play the game the way he thinks it should be played.

I have observed the same kind of scene in nursery schools. In both situations a familiar response by mother or teacher is to try to resolve the situation by having the "attacker" apologize to the "victim". "Say you are sorry!" is what you may hear, especially if the mother of the striker-outer is the one on the scene.

It is a common reaction to feel that a child must be chastised and corrected in order to be taught appropriate social behavior. Mothers are often chagrined, feeling that their children's behavior reflects poorly on them. It is certainly true that our goal is to help children learn how to express how they feel about something in a way that does not hurt or offend someone else. And it is also true that these kinds of episodes are good teaching moments. The question is whether being made to apologize helps children learn what we want to teach.

How does it feel to have to say you are sorry if you feel that you are the one who was wronged? Whether you were actually wronged is not the point. Feeling that way and being made to apologize just means that your side of the story has not been heard or understood, so now you feel doubly wronged. If a child complies under duress, neither the cause of the conflict or a better way to resolve such conflicts has been addressed. It doesn't feel fair, and the usual outcome is even more anger and resentment.

An apology empty of genuine feeling is quite meaningless. To mean it requires empathy—the ability to know and identify with how the other person feels. At times that ability can even help you put your own feelings aside for the moment. We call the person who can do that, empathic.

The capacity for empathy is present in children very early on. You can see very young children try to comfort another child who is upset. Often children will reflect the upset of others by becoming upset themselves. Observing in nursery schools, I have seen how a child crying when his mother leaves reminds other children of their own feeling of loss and they then begin to cry, too.

Empathy, like many other abilities, develops as children mature. We play an important part in that development by helping children become aware of the feelings of others. But first, we have to show empathy for *their* feelings. Mothers sometimes will say, "How do you think it made him feel when you did that?" But a child whose own feelings have not been addressed is not ready to think about how someone else feels. It is by understanding and clarifying for our children what they themselves are feeling that they can begin to identify with what others might be feeling.

Insisting that a child apologize as a means of reparation for behavior he thinks was justified simply says to him that you are taking the other child's side, or that you care more about the other child than you do about him. Besides, since the apology is not sincere, the message is that using empty words is the way to gloss over conflict. In fact, one can hear children saying, "I'm sorry", in a somewhat mechanical way if another child complains about his behavior to an adult in charge.

Conflicts between children are most often caused by both, not just one. They arise because children have not yet mastered social interactions and negotiating conflict. They also have not yet mastered the control of their emotions necessary to express feelings in words rather than physically. That is why conflict situations do make for such good teaching moments.

First of all, we can help clarify for a child what it was that happened. "You were angry because he took the toy you were playing with". Or, "You wanted her to play the game your way". In doing that we are both acknowledging our own child's feelings and also making a connection between the feeling and the way it was expressed. Having acknowledged the feeling we can now talk about better ways to express it.

But the next step is to help children figure out how to resolve the conflict. A major problem with the empty apology is that it doesn't teach children how to do that—and that is really what they need to learn. Whether it is by sharing, taking turns, or compromising on the rules of the game, they often need the help of an adult while learning.

"I'm sorry", sometimes may be useful to say last, but almost never, first.

Aggression

Recently I heard two different concerns from two mothers about two different children. One mother was worried about her son being aggressive toward other children. The other mother was concerned about her daughter *not* being aggressive enough. Aggression seems to be something we feel two ways about—we admire it in some situations and don't like it in others.

Of course aggression can have two different meanings. Sometimes it implies hostile behavior, while at other times we use it to mean being self-assertive. We want children to be able to assert themselves, to use initiative and imagination. What we don't want is for them to assert themselves through behavior we don't like. But we also seem to be concerned if they are not self assertive enough. Mothers sometimes find themselves giving two messages: don't hit or attack others, but "stand up" to others who take your toys away, and fight back if you are hit.

Part of the strong reaction to aggressive behavior in young children comes from looking at it through an adult lens. Mothers have often expressed to me the fear that a child who seems to be striking out at others may become a bully, or who knows what else by the time he is older. In their minds, hitting or pushing another child is transformed into adult behavior, and seems to call for a harsh adult response.

In fact, in young children, much of this behavior is simply part of social learning. For aggressive behavior can have somewhat different meanings at different stages of development. Toddlers who are not yet speaking often make social approaches by holding onto another child's hair, or grabbing at a face. They are interested in making contact and haven't yet learned that their friendly intent won't be interpreted that way.

Young children are not at all clear about "yours" and "mine". If a toy is lying nearby, you just take it to play with. Even if another child is holding something that you want to use, a struggle may ensue to take it. Children who are not yet adept at social approaches sometimes try to enter the play of other children in ways that seem aggressive. A child may knock down another child's building, or take a piece of a game someone is playing.

If we understand the meaning of this behavior, it gives us a way to help children become more successful in getting along with others. Just reprimanding children doesn't solve the problem. We need to teach them better ways to achieve their goals.

Children are often not at all clear themselves about what went wrong in interactions with others. For example, we can help a child who is being disruptive to the play of others by clarifying for him and even for the others, that he really would like to join them, and then if possible, help accomplish that outcome.

In the same way, if we want to teach children about sharing, we really have to help to bring it about. If two children want to play with the same toy, we need to make sure they each get their turn. If we want to teach our children to respect the rights of others, we have to be clear about protecting their rights as well. On the other hand, when children take things from each other, that may offer us an opportunity to help children learn the added benefit that can come from playing with something together.

Children striking out at others in anger may need a different kind of learning. Mothers often say to me, "I know he understands, why does he keep doing that?" Controlling the impulse to strike out when one is angry or frustrated is an ongoing struggle of development that continues well beyond acquiring words and understanding the words of others. Sometimes it is a struggle even for adults—think "road rage".

Of course it is because loss of control seems dangerous that mothers have anxiety about children's aggressive behavior. When children express their anger in direct and primitive ways, it can make us feel angry in turn. Our own anger feels scary because an adult's loss of control might have serious consequences. Mothers have told me they at times have even worried about hurting their own children when they are so angry they feel out of control themselves.

But our children are not us. Most of us have developed the ability to control our impulses, and we can help our children while they are developing those controls. In some situations, that may mean actually providing the control they lack. It may mean being proactive, being alert to situations that we know will cause difficulty for a child. It also may mean removing a child from a situation that is too hard for him to remain in. When possible, what can be most helpful is addressing the situation that prompted the angry response to begin with.

In responding to aggressive behavior, it may help to remember that both anger and aggression play an important part in developing independence, in growing up and eventually separating from parents. The challenge for us as parents is to support our children's developing capacity for self-assertion, while teaching acceptable ways of expressing it.

More About Happiness

A reader sent me a long comment in which he disagreed with what I had written in a previous post. I welcome comments and disagreements in general. Hearing pros and cons helps everyone think. In this case it made me think that perhaps I had not been clear enough in what I was saying, and that it might be helpful to expand and hopefully to clarify some of the points I was making.

In his comment, the reader writes, "It has not been my experience that 'children are always going to dislike what parents expect of them'. I would expect this if I expected things of them that were in conflict with their nature and temperament, but not if I encouraged them in ways that were harmonious with those qualities." He is disagreeing with the sentence in my post that he has quoted here.

I think my sentence is misleading. I really do not mean that children are always going to dislike what parents expect of them. Rather, there are always going to be things parents expect that children won't like. For me, the key sentence is the one that follows: "giving up childish pleasures in order to become a social being is not easy."

From infancy on parents play an important part in leading children on to next steps in development. A mother tries to determine if her child is ready to give up the bottle or breast, if he can handle utensils, if she is ready for toilet training, if he is ready to be moved from the crib to a big bed. It is not always clear when it is time to expect that these steps can be taken. Children's reactions to such changes can be confusing.

As children grow, develop language and cognitive skills, they assert their wishes more clearly and their resistance to parents' wishes and expectations may become more direct. At times, as with two year olds, the big NO! may be part of the beginning push for autonomy. What comes with that is ambivalence about dependence and independence, the wish to be taken care of by mommy while also wanting to be free of her constraints. Children often want to do the things they find more pleasurable than following certain routines, or doing their homework. There are times when we would all rather goof off than be responsible. Parents have the job of helping their children move toward being more, rather than less responsible.

The fact is that living with other people, first in a family and then in the world, means that we have to give up some of our own needs and wishes and begin to consider the needs and wishes of others. This is often not easy to do and there are going to be conflicts along the way between parents and children, just as there are between adults. In raising children the challenge is twofold. The first challenge is to determine what is reasonable to expect of our child at any given point in development. The second, is to express these expectations in a way that promotes cooperation rather than conflict.

What makes this difficult is that children are all so different from each other, and there are no hard and fast rules or timetables. We may have general guidelines about children's development but each child marches to his or her own drummer. We have to know our own child. Where we get into trouble is by following some manual, or the "expert" who says the baby should be weaned by this age, or toilet trained by that age.

But using our own judgment and knowledge of our child is also difficult because children's behavior can often be confusing. If a child refuses milk after you have stopped the bottle does that mean she still needs the bottle? If he refuses to use the potty does that mean you started toilet training too soon, or are using the wrong method?

If an older child refuses to go to bed should he just be allowed to stay up? If she won't get dressed on time for school in the morning does that mean something is wrong, or does she need to be disciplined? If he wants an extra half hour of tv is that okay? The fact is that aside from matters of health and safety it is not always clear when we need to stand firm on our requests and when to recognize that something is so important to our child that we need to compromise on our own wishes.

This still leaves us with the question of how to set our expectations in ways that promote cooperation rather than conflict. I think many parents get stuck here trying to use power as a solution, which leads to resorting to punishment. Conflicts then escalate and end in a no win situation at best.

Which takes us back to the matter of happiness. In working with parents I have found that because it is difficult to determine which expectations are reasonable, and because children often protest in unreasonable ways, children's seeming happiness or unhappiness can too easily become the guide that parents use. As parents, we don't like it when children are angry at us or seem unhappy over what we ask of them.

In an ideal world children and parents would cooperate happily. In the real world we have to question whether children's happiness is the best measure of whether or not we are on the right track in what we expect of them.

Really Smart?

A college Freshman I know was assessing his various classes. He mentioned in passing that his roommate sleeps late and never goes to class. When I questioned that, the answer I got was, "Oh, but he is *really* smart!" Apparently this meant that he reads the book, or the lectures on line, and then aces the tests.

Another young man who has been very successful academically shrugged off any praise or credit he might be given by saying he just works hard. "I have classmates who are *really* smart. I'm not, so I know I have to work harder to get these results." In his mind working hard was not as praiseworthy as being innately very smart.

What do these young people mean by "really smart"? In the first instance, the student referred to has the kind of memory that retains just from reading the information needed for tests. He reads the material before the exams and then gives it back as required. (Doing well on tests is also a skill.) But one might question if this is what is meant by education, and what the end result of this process might be.

The other young man quoted was referring to an ability to grasp certain material easily—or so it seemed to him. Not so much remembering facts, as seeming more readily to understand complicated ideas or concepts. Undoubtedly, there are people who seem naturally to excel in one area of study or another. But while their success may seem effortless to others, that is rarely the case.

What is striking, however, is the attitude expressed in both these examples that having to work hard means you're not really smart, and conversely, if you are really smart you don't have to put that much effort into your success. Being smart is more valuable and praiseworthy than having to put in real effort. This seems to be a rather widespread attitude.

A father of a much younger child told me that he realized recently that he was not helping his daughter by praising her to the skies for any small achievement. He saw that she was starting to believe she should immediately excel at anything she tried, whether in sports or academics. As new tasks became more challenging she was starting to feel inadequate when she didn't immediately succeed. Unrealistic praise was having the opposite effect of its intention.

If anyone still remembers, the Chinese Tiger mother criticized American parents for being overly concerned about their children's self-esteem. I think of one of my teachers during my professional training saying that the pleasure a mother takes in her child's accomplishments is an emotional nutrient for the child. I have since observed that the feedback this gives to the child's growing sense of self is as important as vitamins are to the growth of the body.

Of course, the opposite is true too. If we convey the idea that a child is not living up to expectations, that message is received as well. Children may too readily take this to mean that they don't have the "right stuff" and that there is no point in trying.

When our children begin to be transformed from infants to people, we burst with pride and excitement at each new development. When they sit, stand, take their first step, begin to talk, we marvel at each new accomplishment, as if each child reinvents the wheel. On the other hand, when they begin to walk, we don't believe or suggest they could or should run in the marathon. Neither do we tell them they are geniuses when they begin to learn to read.

Hopefully, the message we give is that they have taken a step towards achieving a goal—sometimes an important step—and that in time by taking one step after another they can reach their destination. That is a hard message to deliver in the current climate when achievement is measured by test results rather than by the true acquisition of knowledge. This helps promote the idea that those who are good at learning for the test are "really smart", just as the teachers who successfully teach for the test may be considered really good.

Perhaps as parents, the solution lies in being realistic with our children—as well as ourselves—both in our praise and our encouragement. We can show them how each step they have taken fits into a process of achieving what they are trying to accomplish. At times it can be helpful to remind them where they have come from as well as where they hope to go. Even if they don't get there, by continuing to try they can get closer to the goal.

Many studies have shown that children and adults, too, who believe that they can affect the outcome of what happens to them, are more successful in many situations than those who think that things are outside of their control. We can help our children learn that the effort they make is really part of being "really smart".

"If Only . . ."

Have you ever said, or heard another adult say, "If only my mother had made me practice", or "If only my parents hadn't let me drop that?" We often seem to have regrets about things we didn't do as children, whether learning to play a musical instrument or mastering a sport. Somehow these regrets always seem to end by blaming our parents, as if it were up to them to "make" us do certain things. Does anyone say, "I should have worked harder"?

A young boy I know who is a talented musician, by choice attended a music camp with rules about practicing time which were strictly enforced. The whole set-up sounded to me a little like a self-imposed prison. When he returned I joked with him a little about it and asked how it had worked out. He said it wasn't that bad, and the results he got on his instrument made it all worthwhile.

I was so impressed with that statement, with the connection he was making between the effort and the result. It was also an acceptance of the idea that to play the way he wanted to play required real work on his part. He was willing to do the work in order to get that result.

I have thought a lot about that conversation because so many children these days have difficulty with the relationship between input and outcome. They seem to expect to be able just to know things without learning them, to do things without ever having done them. Having to work at mastering something seems almost to imply that something must be wrong—either with them or with what is being expected of them. Either way, the feeling seems to be that it should not be necessary to work hard, or to struggle with something in order to be able to do it or know it.

Often, children use as their models those who are experts, star athletes, or musicians, or artists. It looks so easy when the basketball player sends the ball through the hoop, or the man up at bat hits a home run. When the piano teacher plays a piece it sounds so good—that must be how it will sound when the child tries it. Disappointingly, it doesn't.

On a holiday at a lake, I saw a child waiting impatiently for her turn to try water skiing. She was totally confident that she would just get right up and ski—it looked so easy when others did it. When that didn't happen, she was outraged and had a meltdown, looking for all the reasons that someone had done something wrong. She could not be persuaded that this was something that would take practice and many tries.

From the time they are very young, children are learning new skills and developing mastery of their environment. They learn how to walk and talk, to dress themselves and tie their shoelaces. Later on they learn how to read and write. All of these skills contribute to their further ability to become self-sufficient and ultimately autonomous individuals. Some of these skills take longer to master than others. Some children have more difficulty mastering certain skills than do others.

You can see with two year olds in particular the frustration children experience when they are having difficulty with something they are trying to do. I always say about two year olds that their reach exceeds their grasp. What they want to do, and what they think they can do, is not matched as yet by what they are capable of doing. Parents frequently relate how children have meltdowns when they can't get something to work the way they want it to.

When children are that young, we sometimes have to protect them from their own ambitions by helping them move on from something that is too hard. At other times, when they calm down we can help them accomplish what they are trying to do—in effect teaching them how to achieve their goals. As children get older, however, we may become impatient with their meltdowns, and those become the issue rather than the underlying problem that may be causing them.

Sometimes the problem may be the expectations that are being set for them, at other times their own expectations of themselves. In either case, what is missing is an understanding of the process of mastering something, the relationship between teaching, learning, practicing and gradual mastery.

Learning something takes work, and is not always fun. It may be that all the contemporary technology: television, computers, ipads—all the gadgets that are intended to make many things easier—also give the message that everything is supposed to be easy. All that passive learning that takes place from early childhood on has replaced active effort.

Perhaps our job as parents is to support children—as we do when they are two—through the step by step process of learning. Whether it is with homework, riding a bike, throwing a ball, or practicing an instrument, helping them to take that next step when they get stuck, our support along the way when it gets hard, can help children not give-up.

Maybe we can prevent another generation of grown-ups saying, "If only . . . ."

Sticky Stickers

Recently, a mom told me that her son was being given stickers in school for each period he behaved well. The boy is in nursery school and has been having some difficulty with impulse control, at times pushing or striking out at another child. I asked her if the stickers were helping the situation. She said that she didn't think they were helping him control himself, but he seemed to be using them as a means of judging himself. She wasn't sure if that was good or bad.

Good or bad—stickers are a sticky question. The question about using stickers comes up often as a means of motivating children to accomplish certain goals. Sometimes this has to do with taking certain developmental steps like toilet training. A sticker is the reward for each success. Sometimes it is intended as a reward for things not done, as with this boy, not hitting. The question, at times, is also raised as a way of getting children to comply with routines, such as dressing themselves, or cleaning up their rooms.

The basic idea in all of these is that a sticker is a reward to children for doing what adults want them to do, and that rewards are a way to *get* children to do what we want them to do. In a way, this idea is the opposite of time-out. Whatever the original theory behind time-out, in practice it has become punishment as a way of achieving compliance by children. So it seems that sometimes—especially if we feel stuck—we turn to reward or punishment as a solution.

Of course, rewards are a more benign approach than punishment, so they may seem like a more desirable solution. But in fact, the two approaches are alike in certain ways. They both rely on consequences—one negative, the other positive—in an attempt to modify children's behavior. Most significantly this is true when it comes to issues of self-control, and developmental readiness to meet adult expectations. If a child is experiencing difficulty in achieving inner control because of a developmental immaturity, such as the boy described earlier, or perhaps needs more time to mature in certain areas, neither reward or punishment will solve that issue. The same is also true when there are other factors causing the behavior that are not being understood. Reward and punishment don't address those kinds of issues.

But what about stickers? Don't they help children feel good about themselves, and isn't that a motivator for behavior? Yes and no. Children enjoy having stickers and like the idea of being rewarded. What often happens, though, is that when the novelty wears off, children lose interest and the stickers rather quickly lose the power they may have seemed to hold over behavior.

Another outcome that I hear about a lot is that children want the stickers whether they have "earned" them or not. Conflict ensues between parent and child over whether a child's behavior was deserving of the sticker. Needless to say there can be a big difference of opinion between them about that. Now a second area of conflict is added to whatever the original issue was about problem behavior.

What about the idea of rewards for things children need to accomplish as part of life? Suppose the reward was money rather than stickers. Should we pay children each time they go to the potty, or dress themselves, or brush their teeth? That may seem ridiculous, but in fact whether it's money or stickers, basically what we are saying is that the reason for doing things is to get a reward.

Actually, reward initially *is* a motivating factor in children's behavior. The reward they get for appropriate behavior is the approval of mom and dad. That is more satisfying than the disapproval they receive when parents are displeased. But the goal in raising our children is that they will develop those standards within themselves and take responsibility for their own behavior even when no parent or other adult is looking. The reward lies in becoming an independent individual who can function well on one's own.

The mom I referred to earlier was concerned that her son was measuring himself, as she put it, by the stickers. The stickers were telling him whether he had been "good" or "bad". He was not really in touch with his own behavior—only with what the stickers told him. Aside from the fact that they were not helping him manage his behavior, it's not clear what standards the teacher was using when judging his behavior.

Perhaps the main problem in using stickers to change behavior is that it sidesteps addressing whatever it is that is interfering with a child's mastery of the behavior change we're after. The implied assumption seems to be that a child could do it if he wanted to, and the stickers will make him want to. But if our own expectations are off, stickers won't change that. If a child is defiant or rebellious toward authority, stickers won't solve that problem either.

Children may certainly enjoy a sticker as a sign that we recognize something well done or a big step taken. But as a means of bringing about that step, stickers don't stick.

Helping Children Learn

Some time back I wrote about children not making the connection between mastering something and the work it takes to get there. They often think they should know something without having learned it. What they miss is the process of learning—that knowing something or being able to do something is the result of a process which may go smoothly but often has some bumps. If they hit a bump they may too quickly think that means they can't learn it, or do it.

As parents and teachers we, too, may at times forget that learning is a process. Hopefully, at the end of that process children will be where too often we want them to be at the start. A new school year will be starting soon, and each year I have the privilege of talking to a group of teachers about the year ahead. I always try to remind them that the new group of children will not be starting where the old group left off. At the end of the previous year it was such a pleasure to see how far the children had come. But the new group is at the beginning, not at the end of that road.

Of course, as parents we are not dealing with a new child each year. We do sometimes have to remind ourselves with a younger child that she is not in the same place as her older sibling, and also that her way of learning may differ. But each of our children is continuing to move forward from where he or she is now, rather than where either was a year ago.

At times it may seem from children's behavior that they are moving backward, not forward. It can be frustrating when we thought our children had mastered something, only to find it "unlearned". That can happen sometimes after a summer break or other vacation, a stressful event, even an illness. It can be harder to be patient when we believe a child already knows how to do something and isn't doing it. Our expectation changes and so does our attitude.

But at times this seeming to move backwards, or staying in the same place, happens when children hit one of those bumps in learning. They get stuck, and because the next step is not coming easily they conclude it is too hard, or it's something they're not good at, or they are not able to learn it. This is when they think they should just know something without the work of learning it. Often their way of handling that is to give up, to put their attention elsewhere, to resist the task at hand, or to act silly or babyish.

A challenge of teaching, in a classroom or as a parent, is to help children over these bumps. In meeting this challenge, one of the things I have found most helpful to remember is that nothing succeeds like success. Being successful and feeling successful is a great motivator for sticking with something. That's what can dispel the idea that "I'm just not good at this", or "I can't do this". So how can we help a child be and feel successful when he seems not to be getting something?

Too often we do this by trying to pull or push the child forward when actually we need to go back. We need to go back to the place where he had mastered a previous step and was doing it successfully. I've seen how this works with children who are learning to read, or play an instrument, or master a sport skill. You may hear a child say, "That was easy", after doing something he knows how to do. An adult may feel that it is meaningless if a child just does what was "too easy" for him.

Actually, it is that feeling of being successful that can help a child be willing to try a next step. After all, what seems easy now may not have started out that way. If he or she wants just to stay at that good place for a while, that's o.k. too, as long as we remember to use that success to lead gradually to what comes next. And, hopefully, not to make the next step one that is too big for a given child's stride.

The same thing is true as it relates to behavioral mastery. From the very beginning, whether it is giving up the bottle, toilet training, using utensils, dressing oneself, or any other developmental step, there may be regressions or resistance to taking a next step along the way. We can't let our own changed expectation get in the way of going back to an earlier stage that was successful in order eventually to move forward once again.

Although not as monumental as a moon landing, one small step for a child may be a giant step in learning.

CONFLICTS

Confrontation

NO! The most dangerous word in the English language—or any language for that matter—for parents and children. When children say it, mom's hackles are raised. When parents' say it, children are ready for battle. "No," is definitely a no-win strategy with children.

A reader made an interesting comment in response to an earlier post on anger, which illustrates this issue. Mom writes about her five year old: "I'll say 'No juice before dinner', and he'll say, 'Yes!' and march over to the fridge and get it. I'm stuck in the moment: if I let it go, he gets the impression he doesn't have to listen. If I don't let it go, I'm in for a one to two hour battle I may not have the time and energy for."

This is a dilemma familiar to many parents. What is at work is the feeling that the child's defiance (or disobedience) has to be stopped immediately, and that the only two possibilities are "his way or my way." Along these lines another reader comments: "What's the fine line between tolerance (of a child's anger) and promoting the idea of having respect for one's mother or father?"

Although two different points are being made in these comments, they both reflect the idea that if the child's (mis)behavior does not take priority, the consequences will be undesirable—or unacceptable. Challenges to parental authority seem to call for an immediate response, and that response most often is to try to stop and/or correct the behavior rather than to try to address what is behind it. Now the stage is set for a confrontation and power struggle—as our reader says, " . . . a one to two hour battle".

Why do we think that the heat of emotion makes for a teachable moment—when often what we're feeling is, "it's time to teach him a lesson", which has a very different meaning. The idea of responding to what is behind the child's behavior instead of trying to stop or correct it, can mistakenly feel as though we are doing nothing about it.

Let's think about that. In the example of the five year old and the juice, his behavior sounds like defiance. Although he *is* defying his mother's authority, he is also saying something about himself: "I am a big strong boy and don't need your permission because I can do things myself." He is at a stage where autonomy is important to him, and his mom's "No" feels like an attack on his own sense of self. He's ready to do battle to defend it.

Does that mean that mom is supposed to let him do whatever he wants? Of course not. But it does mean that if she understands where his behavior is coming from, that understanding can give her some better idea of how to respond to him. Clearly, trying to be the boss at this moment is not going to be productive.

A five year olds' feeling that he no longer needs his mother is obviously unrealistic. Not only does he need his mother, she is also responsible for him. But there is a difference between being in charge, and acting like "the boss". The lesson she needs to teach him relates to the other comment quoted earlier: about respect. He needs to learn to respect her wishes.

This is not something that can be taught and learned in one encounter—and with young children there will be no shortage of learning opportunities! It would be so nice if our children just did what we wanted them to do because we said so. But it doesn't work that way. As they grow and develop, our children begin to spread their wings and assert themselves. And let's not forget that in many ways we want that to happen. They have to be able to fly off on their own one day!

What we want our children to learn is that they need to respect our wishes not because we are bigger, stronger and more powerful—that won't always be the case, anyway. The real reason is that mutual respect is what enables people to live together without constant, unpleasant conflict. Our children have to begin to see the connection between the many ways in which we do respect their wishes and the consideration we also expect from them. Learning this is a process, one that is often difficult for both parent and child.

How does this apply to moments of conflict such as the example here? One way might be instead of using the provocative "No", responding to what the child is asking for, while moving things in the direction you want to go. "I hear you, you're thirsty. Let's see if we can find something that will be better to drink before dinner." Also, if you confirm for him that of course he is able to get it himself because he is a big, strong boy, he may be better able to hear that sometimes he has to respect your wishes, just as in other ways you respect his.

This approach may not solve things the first time, or many times after. But we know that learning takes repetition and consistency. Nothing terrible will happen if he defeats your intention by getting the juice himself—unless you *feel* defeated. There will be moments later on to review the episode with him and point out that just because he can do things himself doesn't mean it is always a good idea to do so.

It's hard to step back in the face of a child's defiance. Saying "No" may seem like a shortcut, and may better match the way we feel. But what is gained from a one or two hour battle?

Drawing The Line

The question about finding the balance between freedom and authority seems to strike a chord for many parents. When it comes right down to the everyday issues that arise with children, the answer to "where do you draw the line?" can become quite murky. And parents struggle with this question.

Some examples that mothers often raise: "My daughter has very strong opinions about her clothes and wants to choose what she will wear. I want to give her a choice but she insists on wearing a sleeveless summer dress in the middle of winter and refuses to get dressed in anything else."

Or another favorite: "My son has very definite food preferences and won't eat what I make for dinner if it isn't his choice. He wants me to make something else for him." Or yet another example: "My son wants a video game that other children have but I don't think is appropriate. It's an ongoing battle, and I'm not sure whether I should get it for him or not."

These may seem simply like examples of the conflict between what a mother wants and what her child wants: the familiar sounding, "He wants his own way." But as parents, we often feel conflicted within ourselves about whether we should be giving our children the freedom to make choices, or should be asserting our authority as parents in ending these conflicts. In other words, we are not sure where to draw the line between freedom for our children and our authority as their parents.

Perhaps our difficulty in finding the answer lies in the question itself. Drawing the line sounds too much like drawing a line in the sand. "Don't cross that line or else . . . ." (that's when the Chinese mother's methods begin to rear their ugly heads). Asserting authority seems to suggest a big stick, or dire consequences. And that is just what intensifies the conflict. As one mom told me, she knows she is having trouble with the authority side. So the question of finding the right balance between freedom and authority raises another question: Is there another way to assert authority besides threatening with a big stick?

Part of our problem comes from thinking there is a right answer to every given situation. Should I let my daughter wear her summer dress to school? Should I make a different dish for my son? Should I buy the video game my child wants? If we're thinking of finding the right balance, instead of the right answer, that means using judgment.

Of course as parents we are responsible for our children's health and welfare. That covers summer dresses in winter and video games we deem inappropriate. As far as a different meal at dinner time goes, that depends on how a mom feels about operating a restaurant with a menu. The point is, some things are more clear cut than others, but we shouldn't get mixed up about things that are real choices and those that are our responsibility as parents.

At times parents are clear that there are things children should not be deciding for themselves, but want to avoid the conflict that ensues when either they, or their children, dig in their heels. In other words, we give up and take the path of least resistance, which turns out to be the long way home in the end. But why does a difference of opinion about what to wear turn into such a conflict?

This brings us back to how do we as parents stay in charge? Part of the answer lies in feeling clear within ourselves that we *are* in charge. It's amazing how that feeling of confidence gets communicated to our children in our voice and manner without our sounding like a dictator or making threats.

But, just as important, when we feel confident about our expectations as parents, we can be much more open to hearing our children's point of view. I mean hearing, not capitulating to their point of view. What is so special about that summer dress? Maybe we can find that something special for winter. I'm sorry you didn't like tonight's dinner. What would you like tomorrow? We can help our children feel they are being considered, even when they don't get what they want. And we can be sympathetic rather than defiant about not getting the video that some other children have.

Perhaps that line we're talking about is a wavy line that allows for some give and take. A line, where as the ones in charge, we're not too worried about whether it is being crossed.

The Illusion of Control

A reader made an interesting comment and raised a question in response to an earlier article, "No Fault Mothering." She writes about her five year old who is aggressive toward her nine year old and other family members when he doesn't get the attention he wants. She has told him to use his words, not his hands, and given him time-outs until he apologizes. His response is to pee in his room. She wants to figure out what is going on inside his head and says, "The advantage of making this 'my fault', is that it gives me the illusion of control. If it's my fault, then I can fix it, right?"

This is a most insightful comment. When mothers find something difficult or problematic going on with their children, they tend to see only two alternatives: either something is wrong with the child or with themselves. The idea that something might be wrong with a child is a little scary. Mothers often find it preferable to see it as their fault, feeling that offers the greater possibility of "fixing it".

Our reader calls this "the illusion of control" and she is right about that, because it *is* an illusion—one that is quickly shattered. What happens is that a child's provocative or aggressive behavior that we can't seem to do anything about makes us feel out of control. We feel as though we *should* be able to control such behavior, and when we can't, our feelings of helplessness, frustration and anger often lead to punitive responses that don't help at all. So the idea that one is in control is indeed, an illusion.

A wise teacher once told me, "You're in control if you feel in control". Of course, the question is, how do you get to feel in control? You can start by accepting the fact that you can't control a child's behavior in the sense of *making* him stop doing something. The behavior of young children can be very primitive and cause parents to become primitive in their own responses. Pretty soon both parent and child are out of control, and this kind of confrontation simply leads to more upset and guilt for mom.

Our comment writer is on the right track when she says she needs to figure out what is going on inside her younger child's head. The way to begin is by asking some questions. What is the attention he wants that he feels he is not getting? Why is he so angry at everyone? Does he feel shut out with everyone older and bigger than he is? Is he finding it hard to get the space he needs to be heard? Looking at the situations in which his unacceptable behavior occurs can help you shed some light on it.

The next thing might be to accept the fact that the methods you are using are not doing any good, in fact they seem to be making him angrier (peeing in his room is a pretty angry response). So why continue with them? One of the things that happens in unresolved conflicts is that a pattern of behavior gets set in place. Child does his thing, mom does her thing; everyone follows the same script, and nothing changes. A young child is not capable of being the one to change, so mom has to go first. You have to change your response in order to break into a behavioral pattern that has been established.

How to do that? One way might be, instead of telling him to use his words, tell him that you see he is having trouble learning to use his words and you will help him. The fact is that impulse control is a developmental step which is hard for children to master—harder for some children than for others. It's even hard for some adults. Anger is a big emotion, and the impulse is to strike out. It takes a lot of work to transform that into talk out. Children *do* need help while they are learning to do that.

What about the time-outs until he apologizes? Why is it so important to apologize? Mothers, at times, get very invested in apologies, as if getting a child to apologize for something he has done fixes it. Or at least helps a mother feel that she has done something in response to his behavior. In fact, an apology in this kind of situation accomplishes nothing except to make the child apologizing feel doubly wronged. Whatever the feeling was that made him strike out in the first place has not been addressed, and now he is, in effect, being punished for his feelings. If you want to "figure out what is going on inside a child's head", you have to try to see things from his point of view, not your own. If you want to help him learn that he cannot hurt someone else, first you have to address what is causing him to feel hurt.

The message is, give up the illusion of control and trade it in for trying to understand your child's behavior.

Discipline Is Teaching

In our ongoing "Praise a Parent" campaign, a reader posted an example of praise she offered to a colleague for disciplining her three girls. We don't know the details, but the episode ended with the girls calling their mom "rude", and "the worst mom ever". The reader who offered the example says it sounds as though the mom made "great, though difficult choices" in disciplining, and ends by saying, "Discipline is hard".

This is an excellent example because it points up an important part of being a parent that is more often a source of conflict than of praise. Mothers think about discipline a great deal: when to discipline, how to discipline, even whether to discipline. Discipline is a critical part of a mother's role as teacher, yet it is often a source of confusion because it gets translated as punishment.

The question of discipline is often raised when children's behavior runs counter to parents' expectations or requests. A child "refuses to listen", or is defiant, or behaves in unacceptable ways if he doesn't get what he or she wants. Discipline then becomes a search for a method that will control behavior we don't like, or feel is inappropriate. Parents often talk about this in terms of learning: "She has to learn to do as she is told", or "He has to learn he can't have everything he wants." The question then is, if a child has to learn something, what is the best way to teach it?

Even when talking about teaching and learning, a strong feeling persists in many of us that only punishment will drive a lesson home. People have strong opinions about whether or not punishment is an effective teacher. It's interesting, though, that punishment only comes up as a method of teaching for certain kinds of behavior—behavior that is considered "bad". Few of us would think of punishment as a solution for a child having a hard time learning to tie her shoelaces, or learning spelling, or solving arithmetic problems. We distinguish between academic learning and social learning, yet both involve teaching.

So the question really is, what is an effective way of teaching appropriate social behavior? Maybe we have to start by asking why a child isn't learning. Does he understand what is expected? Is he being expected to do something that he is not yet capable of doing, or Is he being asked to do something he doesn't want to do? Is he defiant because he feels the expectations are unfair? Answering these questions means trying to understand why a child is misbehaving and influences what we do about it.

The problem with punishment is that it doesn't address the underlying reason for the behavior we are trying to change. If a child is having difficulty with self-control, the memory of having been punished is not going to help him control an impulsive expression of his feelings at the moment. If the behavior is defiance, punishment may serve to increase anger and then the defiant behavior. The idea that a child should be punished is usually an expression on our part of frustration about the behavior, and the feeling that it has to be corrected or responded to right then and there.

But if we are to think in terms of teaching and learning, we have to remember that it is a process that takes time, and we may have to take a longer view when it comes to correcting behavior. Of course, that doesn't mean we shouldn't respond to unacceptable behavior. Parents often say, "There has to be a consequence". An important part of growing up is learning that there are consequences to our behavior. If that is so, the consequences need to flow from the behavior, not be something made up that has nothing to do with the behavior. If children are to learn to take responsibility for their behavior, they need to experience the connection between what they do and what the result may be.

For example, if a child dawdles in the morning and won't get dressed, she may have to be late for school and deal with whatever that entails. If she doesn't fulfill whatever responsibility she has at home, that may result in a loss of privilege that goes with being a family member. If she misbehaves in a restaurant when the family is having dinner out, she may have to be taken out, away from the others.

Sometimes the teaching and learning break down because it is too hard, or too inconvenient to see something through with a child when it is actually happening. It becomes easier just to let things slip by, or to threaten consequences that will be implemented later. Instead of teaching as we go along, we may let the behavior go too far and then try to correct it all at once.

The reader who reported the discipline incident ended by saying, "Discipline is hard". She's right. The mom she talked about was called "rude", and "the worst mom ever", by her children. Children often don't like what we are expecting of them. We have to do internal checks to make sure that what we expect is realistic and fair. But we also have to be able to tolerate being "the worst mom ever" when we stick to our expectations.

Needs Or Wants? (Part one)

There is an old joke that says, "When I was a child my parents got the white meat of the chicken. Now that I'm a parent my children get the white meat of the chicken. When will it be my turn?"

Even if the white meat isn't really your preference, this joke does speak to a big change that took place in ideas about parents and children. At one time we thought children were supposed to defer to parents; now parents feel that they are supposed to defer to children And the image of the "good mother" has become one who puts her children's needs first.

This idea has created lots of confusion and worry for mothers. Child development research has told us that beyond the need for physical care, good care means meeting children's emotional and psychological needs. But what are they? And how do you do that? It's not just that the answers given in much child rearing advice keep changing. It's also that trying to apply those answers is often unworkable, because there is no clear cut definition of what a child truly needs in any given real life situation.

A working mom said to me, "I missed a school program my daughter was in and in my mind I was thinking that ten years from now she'll say, 'You know why I'm all screwed up? Because you didn't come to this and this and this'."

Another mother talked about the conflict she was feeling because of a rare opportunity to join her husband on a business trip that would mean leaving her two year old for a week. She wanted to know whether such a separation wouldn't cause terrible problems for her child.

Mothers not only want to do the "right thing" for their children, they worry about the consequences if they do the "wrong thing". But mothers have needs too, and that's where the conflict comes in. This conflict between a mother's needs and a child's needs has intensified for mothers working outside the home, but it exists for all mothers. It goes with the territory, because children are dependent on us and we are responsible for their care.

It may start with something that seems clear cut, like the baby's need to be fed at night conflicting with mom's need for sleep. But even then, mothers sometimes say, "He's just crying because he *wants* to be picked up". We know that babies *do* need to be held (although once upon a time even that was a "no, no"). The point is that even at the beginning, needs and wants can get mixed up.

As children get older, it becomes even more complicated, because they have more ideas and wishes of their own and a greater ability to assert them. In addition, their own needs and wants are their primary focus. Mom is not yet another person who has to be considered. Children feel they *really need* whatever it is they want—and sometimes behave as if their very life depends on it. It is not surprising that mothers get mixed up about what they *need* and what they *want*.

Sometimes, when a conflict arises, a mother feels she has no choice, as with the mom whose job made it impossible for her to attend the school play. Other mothers who work because their work life is important to them, struggle with their feelings of conflict and guilt. But there are so many other situations, like the mom with the trip possibility, where the conflict is between something a mom wants for herself and her fear that she will be damaging her child by failing to meet his needs. Is the child's need for mom greater than her need to do something for herself? Children, of course, think the answer to that is yes. But that doesn't make it so.

What we are really confronting here is a fundamental question in all relationships. When two people have conflicting needs, how do you decide which is more important? Mothers tend to look for the "right" answer that will resolve the conflict. The problem is that there is no "right answer". There is no rule that can tell a mother whether staying with her child is more important than going on a trip with her husband. There is no way for a mother to know with certainty what the consequences will be of missing the school play.

One of the hardest things about raising children is that these conflicts are ongoing and have to be thought through each time. The mom conflicted about the trip has to think through what she knows about her son, how he has been dealing with separations, who will stay with him while she is gone, and are there ways she can prepare him for her absence. Most important, she has to accept the idea that he may be angry with her when she returns, and express that anger in behavior that makes life difficult for her. (A credit card company once had an ad that said "travel now, pay later".) But none of that means that she shouldn't go with her husband. The importance of the trip for her and for her marriage is the other part of the equation.

The main point is that both this mom and the one who missed the school play have to make these decisions based on their knowledge of their own situation—not on some theoretical "right" thing to do. The most important thing they can do is to be ready to help their children deal with whatever their feelings are in response to mom's decisions. Children *can* survive frustration. If you help them master it, you will help them grow.

Needs or Wants? (Part two)

A Mom talking to me about her daughter said, "Sometimes she wants too much. She can be demanding. She can get over-demanding. But I'm not sure if I should say that because then I feel guilty and think well, I'm at work and I shouldn't say she is over-demanding. But I think she is because I can't do it and she is always asking. So you really don't know because the requests are coming in faster than you can meet them."

This Mom was really trying to figure out if her daughter's requests were justified. Was she asking for what she needed or for what she wanted? Partly the Mom feels angry at her daughter asking for things Mom can't do, and that makes her feel her daughter is "over-demanding". But that makes Mom feel guilty about the fact that she is working, and she worries that maybe her daughter really needs what she is asking for. She worries that maybe it is her own fault she is not able to meet these requests.

There is another part to the confusion about needs and wants that is expressed in what this mother is saying. She is trying to determine if the requests are legitimate as a way of deciding whether her daughter is "*over*-demanding". Another word someone might use is "spoiled". So the implication is that one of them is at fault; either Mom is to blame for not being able to meet the requests, or her child is to blame for asking.

This is a very common response to conflict, not just between mother and child, but between people in general. We often try to resolve a conflict by asserting that one person is right and the other wrong, one position is justified and the other one isn't. In the example here, if the daughter is *over*-demanding then Mom is justified in not meeting her requests and does not have to feel guilty.

Even without realizing it, trying to decide if something is a need or a want seems to be part of the process mothers go through in responding to their children. It's as if needing something makes it o.k. but wanting it is not. Many mothers today are struggling with the feeling that their children are over-demanding. There is a kind of moral judgment that wanting things is bad.

Children want lots of things. Most of the conflicts between mothers and children are over a child wanting something mom can't do, doesn't want to do, or feels it inappropriate or unwise to do. Like the mom quoted, mothers may at first feel that the requests are acceptable, but then start to feel angry with their children for asking. Many mothers describe a scene in which a child's escalating requests lead not only to mom's "no", but an insistence that the child learn he is wrong for asking.

There is nothing wrong with children wanting things. There is nothing wrong with mom not giving a child everything he wants. The problem comes when a child gets mom's anger and the message that he is "bad" for wanting. The child then gets angry in turn and lets mom know he thinks she is bad for saying no. That's when a simple conflict turns into a conflagration.

Sometimes we unwittingly participate in this kind of escalation because it may be easier to just say yes. Nobody likes dealing with a child's protests—which sometimes come in the wrong place at the wrong time. But what seems like the easier path often turns out to be more difficult in the end. From the child's point of view, increasing his protests may seem like the way to go. mom and child end up in a tug of war in which one or the other may feel defeated, but in which no one really wins.

It's not surprising that children protest when they don't get what they want. When you stop to think about it, so much of what a child is required to do is what mom wants and he doesn't: "go to bed", "get dressed", "wash hands", "stop playing", "no more tv"—and lots more besides not getting what he wanted at the store. "Why do I always have to do what mom wants?" You could sympathize with his plight if his objections weren't making life more difficult.

In the conflicts that arise, children are not only seeking to gratify their wishes, but also struggling to be in charge of things over which they have very little control. Understanding that can help us be more sympathetic in our responses. It's hard not to get what you want. But sometimes it's hard not to give it. And that's when we get angry at children for asking.

"Traitor's Throat"

Years ago there was a funny book called "What Dr. Spock Didn't Tell Us". In it, a new father describes and names behavior of children that the "experts" don't tell you about. One he calls "Traitor's Throat": what a baby has when she cries just loud enough to wake up her father but not loud enough to wake up her mother. He can lie there half the night waiting to see if she won't wake up her mother—but she never does!

Of course there are many mothers who would agree with the name but question the description. They would say they are the ones who hear the baby's cries while dad sleeps on. "Traitor's Throat" at times seems to be a symbol of the division of labor that evolves between couples when they become parents.

What evolves may not be what couples planned ahead of time. In this day and age, when in so many families both parents work outside the home, sharing of responsibilities is a big issue. In fact, these days, more is expected of fathers even when mothers are home full time. Still, couples are usually unprepared for the way life is transformed by children, and the ways in which reality differs from expectations.

Much has been written and discussed about the pressures women face as mothers working outside the home. Despite the increased involvement of fathers, it often seems as though women have the ultimate responsibility for managing the home and childcare. Symbolically—and often realistically—it's mom, not dad, who hears the child's cries. Or as many mothers have said, "Who does the school call if the child is sick?"

There are, of course, many reality factors that impact on who does what. Work schedules, the nature of respective jobs, and the degree of work flexibility, among other things. But often there are other issues at play which are not always so clear cut, as parents try to address questions of responsibility.

A mother and father came to see me about some difficulties they were having with their son's bedtime and other routines. The conflict between them had to do with expectations for the child's compliance to their requests. Dad felt that mom was too impatient and that he got better results by giving the child more time. Mom disagreed and felt she allowed plenty of time before drawing the line.

When we explored the conflict between them further, it seemed clear that what was behind mom's seeming lack of patience was the pressure she was feeling from work and family responsibilities. She had no time for herself or her own needs. Dad expressed his frustration at this because he always offered to take their son out on weekends and his offer was always rejected. Dad saw this as a lack of Mom's confidence in him as a father, and was angry at his wife's feeling that he was not supportive. How could he be supportive if she rejected his concrete offers of help?

What was this really all about? As it turned out, Mom was not asking for concrete help. The problem for her was that she had so little time to spend with her child that she both wanted and felt she ought to give her son whatever time she herself was not away at work. She did not feel she had the right to give to herself something she needed. By supportive, she meant emotional support. She wanted her husband to understand the pressure she felt, so he would not be critical of her if she lost it at times with their son. Dad was completely amazed by this. He had been trying to solve what he saw as the problem in a way that made sense to him. Unfortunately, they were not on the same page.

In writing about conflicts with our children, what often comes up is the need to think about where a child is coming from—to see things from his or her point of view. To "hear" what he or she is saying, or asking. And the same is true of relationships between adults. We all come from different realities and, therefore, see things differently. We often think that the way *we* see things is the true reality—that we are right and the other person is wrong. This is what leads both children and adults to feel that they have not been heard. Perhaps many of us have difficulty with this because we did not have the experience of being heard in that way when we ourselves were children.

It is not always easy to understand what another person is really telling us. Children don't yet have the words or the means to tell us what they want or feel, and so express themselves in behavior that is often unpleasant. We have to get over our dislike of their behavior in order to think about what they are really saying.

But this can be true of us as adults, too. Sometimes we ourselves are not clear about what we really mean but can be helped to express it more clearly when the other person is ready to listen. We can help our children in the same way.

Truly hearing each other not only enables us to be more effective in responding to our children, it provides an important model for them as they learn to deal with conflict.

Are Chinese Mothers Superior?

Have you been following the furor caused by Amy Chua's book, BATTLE HYMN OF THE TIGER MOTHER? The book is basically an indictment of Western (read American) mothers, comparing them unfavorably to Chinese mothers. She attributes the impressive number of math and music prodigies the Chinese produce to their model of parenting, which includes coercive strictness, punishment and shaming.

In an essay in the Wall Street Journal, ("Why Chinese Mothers are Superior", 1/8/11) Ms. Chua says the success of Chinese mothers is due to three major differences between "Chinese and Western parental mind-sets": first, Western parents are extremely anxious about their children's self-esteem and worry too much about how their children will feel if they fail at something. Chinese parents demand perfect grades because they believe their children can get them—and if they don't, it's because they didn't work hard enough.

Second, Chinese parents believe their kids owe them everything and therefore must spend their lives repaying their parents by obeying them and making them proud.

Third, Chinese parents believe they know what is best for their children and therefore override all of their children's own desires and preferences.

What is most interesting is the intense response this thesis has brought about. Comments from readers and reviewers range from condemnation to approval. Ms. Chau's point of view seems to have touched a nerve among American parents and educators. The intensity of their reaction, both pro and con, suggests that some deeply held beliefs are being challenged. But it also suggests that American parents are worried about whether these beliefs are leading to the results they have hoped for.

What is this really all about? The heart of the matter seems to be different points of view in these two different cultures about conflict between what a mother wants and what her child wants. The goal of the mother is to socialize and promote successful, independent functioning. The goal of the child is to gratify his needs and wishes. What the mother wants interferes with what the child wants, and children react in ways that often make life difficult for parents.

From the description Amy Chau offers, Chinese mothers are ready to use extreme measures, including strict demands, severe punishment, shaming and humiliation, among other things, to achieve their sky-high goals and expectations. Their children's feelings and desires are not an issue to be considered. The parent is the authority in all matters, and children are raised from the outset to defer to that authority. This is all in the service of a certain kind of success.

Ms. Chua writes somewhat contemptuously of "Western" parents' concern for children's self-esteem, feelings, and "psyches". These concerns reflect our values of individualism, self-expression, and the right to question authority. Yet they were not always incorporated into our child-rearing practices.

Looking back on past child-rearing practices in America, we find many similarities to the Chinese model. Americans, too, once believed in parents as *the* authority, and used some of the same methods of enforcement. But in time these beliefs and methods gave way to new theories growing out of child development research.

For example, we went from "picking up babies causes spoiling", to "babies need to be held and comforted"; from rigid feeding schedules to demand feeding; from strict toilet training to following a child's lead; from "children should be seen but not heard", to "children need to express their feelings"; from "spare the rod and spoil the child", to a focus on children's rights. We moved from the parent as authority to the child as authority, and now, unfortunately, to the "expert" as authority.

The problem for American parents is that we really want the results the Chinese mothers are getting, but without using their methods. The difficulties we experience at times with our children's behavior may lead us to question our methods. And if our methods are wrong, maybe there is also something wrong with our beliefs. These are the questions stirred up by Amy Chau's book.

One answer may be that we have gone too far down a certain road. In moving away from practices that damaged children in one way, we have inappropriately given them the sort of control over their own upbringing that creates other kinds of problems. Chinese mothers have a culture and history that support their beliefs and methods. As American mothers we are always looking for, and open to, new ideas and methods. But these ever-changing approaches serve to undermine self-confidence and common sense. The problem lies here, not in our beliefs themselves.

Parents need to re-learn being in charge. This is an attitude and a conviction—not a method.

Working and Mothering

A reader of goodenoughmothering asked for an article on "working and mothering simultaneously". The first thing to point out is that all mothers are working mothers, so the question is really about mothering combined with other employment. We can't even talk any more about stay-at-home mothers and working mothers because so many women have found ways to do other work within the home.

This subject has generated much controversy, especially in the years since more and more women have combined motherhood with work outside the home. It is an emotional topic that has numerous aspects which cause conflicts for many women. The obvious conflict between motherhood and work outside the home relates to child care. The expense, inadequacy and unavailability of child care are a major problem. This is a subject that needs an article in itself.

Despite the gains that have been made in meeting the needs of mothers, the work world is still one designed for a breadwinner/homemaker couple, and its demands conflict with the world of motherhood. Having to straddle these two worlds is a major source of stress. You start to feel that you are shortchanging your children, your work, or both—and forget about having time for personal needs.

But a deeper source of inner conflict for many women comes from our idealization of mother care. The idea that not only do children need a mother's care, but that only a mother can meet her child's needs, is still a very strong belief. Added to that is the emphasis in our culture on individualism and the conviction that individual care is superior care. This adds up to the message that a mother is supposed to take care of her own children and if she is working outside the home they are being shortchanged.

What I have found is that many of the worries mothers have, and the difficulties they may get into with their children, come not from *working* outside the home but from their *feelings* about working away from home. First and foremost is the feeling of guilt that maybe their children's needs are not being met adequately. Whatever the form of child care—including full time mother care—there are always compromises, but mothers think those compromises would not have to be made if they were home.

The worry that maybe a child's needs are not being met often leads to an attempt to compensate in some way, and what children want gets mixed up with what children need. Mothers who are away all day say they don't want to be disciplinarians during the limited time they have with their children. But their wish not to say "no", can lead to too many yeses. Sometimes appropriate expectations, such as bedtime, go by the board.

Mothers who work away from home are quick to attribute any bump in the road with their children to the fact that they are working. There are always going to be conflicts between parents and children as children assert their own wishes, which are often not what parents think is best for them. But if a child seems to be having a hard time with separation, friendships, participating in activities, or other areas of development, mothers are too ready to blame themselves and the fact that they are working.

The problem with this is that it can keep you from looking at what else is going on for a child; either in other parts of his life or in what he may be struggling to master. Is something going on in school? Did she have a fight with a friend? Is something being expected of him that is too hard? Even if it is related to not being there for your child in a particular way, that doesn't mean you shouldn't be working. What more specifically can address the need here? Possibly arranging to go along on a school trip, picking her up from school now and then, having a special time for him, looking at possible sibling issues? There can be several kinds of solutions if you move away from self-blame.

The conflict women feel may be particularly acute when they are working by choice, pursuing a career or work that is especially meaningful to them. It's as though it is somehow wrong to be pursuing something meaningful to you on a personal level when you should be putting your children first. A conflict of needs and/or wishes is inherent in any relationship between people. Historically women have been expected to defer to the needs and wishes of others. In particular, part of the legacy of traditional motherhood is to sacrifice for your children.

The fact is, as long as we value the individual relationship between mother and child, the challenge will be in creating a workable balance in the relationship between the two. Obviously, the younger the child the more required of the mother. But as children grow and mature the balance keeps changing as children learn, too, how to consider the needs of others.

As in everything else, there is no perfect solution to this age old conflict. The answer does not lie in self-sacrifice. But one thing to give up is self-blame.

Choices

Women today seem to have many more choices than did earlier generations. They can choose whether to work or pursue a career, if and when to have a baby, whether to be a stay-at-home mom or to work outside the home, and the kind of child-care to pick if they work. So many choices—or so it seems.

Choice was meant to be liberating. It became the mantra of an earlier generation in the woman's movement. But choice means making a choice, having to choose, within the limits imposed by reality. Choice turns out to be not always as liberating and empowering as everyone had hoped. Choice seems to bring with it many conflicts, both internal and external.

The word one hears more often today is balance. Many women are struggling to meet the many demands made on them—to balance these competing demands. Perhaps the most difficult balancing act has become the one between family life and work. Men as well as women are trying to find that balance. Although perhaps women more than men, both have found that the work world is such that getting ahead—even staying in place—does not permit giving the consideration they would like to give to family life.

Just recently, a judge dismissing claims that a major company had discriminated against new mothers and mothers-to-be wrote, "The law does not mandate 'work-life balance' . . . making a decision that preferences family over work comes with consequences." Here is reality closing in on choice. Combining work and motherhood may mean a limitation on the kind of work that is attainable.

Even the choice to work is in itself not always a choice. Economic reality is such that the need for dual incomes has become a fact of life.

Yet many choices are involved in making that decision, such as where people want to live, what kind of education they choose for their children, what material benefits are important to them. What one values becomes a major issue in the choices made.

Another major reality factor that impacts on the choice to work outside the home is the issue of child-care. In recent years, when finances permit, many women have chosen to give up their work in order to stay home with their children. There are a number of factors involved here including the kind of child-care that is available, but equally important are the feelings of women.

Although some young families are lucky enough to have grandparents or other family members helping out with child-care, the most common choice is between hiring an individual care-giver and seeking some form of group care. Individual care is expensive, difficult to find, and may not meet a parent's standards. Many complicated issues arise between parents and caregivers.

But the quality, affordability and availability of day-care have become controversial issues as well. As soon as you put young children in groups, questions arise as to how many children in a group? How many adults per child? How well trained are the caregivers? How many hours in a center are appropriate for the age of a given child? What is the physical space like? Answering these questions in an acceptable way by definition means higher costs. As a result, all of these factors have limited day-care as an option for many parents.

But the conflict that has arisen for many women in trying to choose the right kind of child-care, or even whether to work outside the home at all, has to do with feelings within themselves. I have written before about the idealization of individual care, and especially mother care, in our culture. We've all been exposed to these beliefs and they permeate our feelings. We fall in love with our babies and are loathe to turn them over to someone else's care. That doesn't mean they can't do well without our being there 24/7. It means that we feel that they won't, and start to feel guilty if we are not there.

These feelings often lead mothers to feel they must give every available hour they are not at work to their children. Not only the realistic demands of work and family, but the kinds of demands they make of themselves can become overwhelming. In many cases, when financially possible this has led to a decision to give up one's work life.

Everyone tries to make the decision that is best for her own situation, but too often what propels such decisions are not just the reality factors, but the conflicted feelings that are stirred up by the choices involved. Conflict within ourselves creates the feeling that something is wrong, or we wouldn't feel this way. We want to rid ourselves of this feeling that causes anxiety, and think that the right decision would take care of it.

As mothers and citizens, there are things that we can work to change, such as better and more available child-care, more parent-friendly conditions in the work place. But conflicted feelings are always going to be with us. They are part of life, because as I hope we have all learned, nothing is perfect. We may choose one thing over another, but that doesn't mean the conflict will be resolved. Instead, we have to learn how to live with contradictory needs and wishes—just as our children do. Choice can be a good thing—as long as we remember that choosing something almost always means also giving something up.

Grandparents: A Mixed Blessing

An old joke says that the reason grandparents and grandchildren get along so well is that they have an enemy in common. Grandparents love to give, children love to receive, and parents may seem to both of them like the enemy of gratification. Mom becomes the one who says, "No", grandma the one who says, "Yes". At least that's what it feels like to the parents.

The mother of a two year old spoke to me recently about feeling stressed by a visit from her husband's parents. In-laws are a subject in themselves, as all the mother-in-law jokes can testify. Although there certainly are important differences in the way parents feel about their in-laws compared to their own parents, their feelings about them as grandparents have many similarities.

Listening to this mother I was struck by the universality of her complaints. Working with parents over many years, I recognize familiar words and themes. But as a grandmother myself, I have also experienced and heard from other grandparents the other side of that same set of feelings. As a friend of mine said, "The grandchildren are wonderful; it's their parents who are the problem."

What I hear a lot from mothers is the feeling of being undermined and criticized by grandma. The mother I refer to above was angry that grandma gave her daughter soda and let her watch tv, two things mom had made clear were not allowed. When the grandmother later said to the child, "Mommy says no," the mother felt she was being made the bad guy, and that this response undermined her authority. The implication (and the reality) was that grandma would allow it—it's mom who won't.

A grandmother I spoke to said, "Our children are so sensitive. They think they're being judged all the time. But actually, they are judging us all the time." Apparently, both mothers and grandmothers each feel judged and criticized by the other. And maybe they are. But what is this really all about?

Many mothers say that while they appreciate the help of grandparents, they have more work afterwards getting their children back to the parents' own rules and routines. But this generational conflict runs deeper than the conventional wisdom that grandparents like being indulgent, while parents have the real responsibility of daily life.

This truism is a surface reality which speaks to the more profound changes that are taking place. Having a child becomes musical chairs in which everyone moves up a place. The child is now the PARENT. Instead of being the child of your parent you are now the parent of your child. Our own feelings of dependency are challenged by having someone who is dependent on us. The feeling of being responsible for another life becomes central.

The idea that one is no longer the CHILD is difficult both for new parents and for their parents. Grandparents may feel that their experienced words of wisdom should be heeded. But when they expect the parents to listen to their advice they are making them children again—which is kind of unnerving when you are trying so hard to be a parent. New parents are working hard to win their parent credentials, while grandparents may be trying to hold on to their own.

In many ways this is a continuation of the developmental process in which children move toward greater independence and struggle to establish their own identity. For parents there is always the question of whether to hold back or to let go. There appears to be a universal impulse to protect one's children, which often becomes trying to keep them from making what seem to parents to be painful mistakes.

Grandparents want their children to learn from their (the grandparents') experience—just as they wanted them to when they were growing up. Parents often are trying to correct the things they think were wrong in their own upbringing. Grandparents get this, and they often take it as a criticism of them. Both parents and grandparents often use the same words in talking about being made to feel incompetent by the other.

Parents are learning how to be parents—just as their parents had to learn. And grandparents have to learn how to be grandparents. That learning is the hardest part. What grandparents can't stand is feeling that the parents are learning at the expense of *their grandchildren*. What is hardest for parents is what they experience as a lack of respect for their role as parents.

Perhaps the important lesson for grandparents is to let their children learn in their own way. For parents who have fond memories of their relationship with their own grandparents, perhaps they can derive comfort from knowing that their children may also have such memories in the years to come.

FEELINGS

"I Need It!

A mom was trying to decide how to respond to the behavior of her two and a half year old son. She described how recently, when he wants something he becomes very emotionally intense and says, "I *need* it, I *really need* it". If he can't have it, he gets very upset and repeats that he "needs it". And no matter what, he really does! Which doesn't mean mom has to give it to him.

This is a beautiful example of young children's deeply felt emotions and the way they express these feelings. When this little boy would like to have something a friend is playing with, or wants an object in the home that is not for playing with—examples the mom gave—he experiences this as "needing" it. It is essential to his sense of well-being at that moment. It is almost as if his life depends on it.

This can be confusing to a parent because from an adult point of view, he doesn't need it, he just wants it. The emotional intensity, and often the behavior that goes with it, doesn't seem justified. We may begin to think in terms of needing to teach him that he can't have everything he wants, which then influences the way we respond.

On the other hand, parents are very sensitive to the idea of meeting their children's needs. One may wonder, why such a strong emotional reaction to what seems like something minor? Does he need something that is being overlooked? Should we give him what he is asking for so he will feel better?

Actually, this goes to the question of what we mean when we think about needs and wants. Have you ever thought, or said, "I need a new pair of shoes to go with that outfit"? That is different from, "My child's shoes are too small, she needs a new pair." Unhappily, there is also "need", as in needing money for food or rent.

So even as adults, we often say "need" when we really mean "want". And even need may mean something not only to make life more comfortable, but also even possible. Think about the times we say need when we really mean want. Even when we don't need something for survival, wanting it may make it feel necessary for our emotional well-being. Hopefully though, as adults we don't have temper tantrums if it's something we can't have.

The difference is that young children have not yet mastered their emotions. Not only that, they also experience things in black and white terms: things are either wonderful or terrible, mom is either the best mom in the world, or the Wicked Witch of the West. So often, when a child wants something, he really feels as though he needs it for his survival.

Of course, he really doesn't need it for his survival. We know that, but he doesn't. Again, that doesn't mean we have to give it to him. What he does need that we can give, is for us to understand that it really feels that way to him. He really believes he won't survive the frustration or disappointment he is feeling. We help him learn that he can and will survive by acknowledging his desperation, and supporting him as he lives through it. This at times may mean riding out the storm with words of comfort rather than criticism.

At other times, however, it may be possible and even desirable to help a child get what he wants. Think about yourself, again. How do you decide whether to indulge yourself with something you want, rather than need? Well, if it's desert and you're on a diet, you may question whether the momentary pleasure is worth the calories. If money is tight, you might question if you can afford it. Or it may come down to a question of priorities, whether what you want in this instance is more important than other things you are hoping to do.

Your child is not yet capable of such rational decision making. Even as adults we sometimes give in to the impulse of the moment—although we may regret it later. The point is, if what the child wants is not unreasonable, why not help him have it? Perhaps the other child will share the toy, or your child can have it next. Perhaps he just wants to touch the object on the shelf rather than play with it. Even if it is something that has to be bought, it might be possible to help him think about whether he wants that toy rather than a different one he has been thinking about.

If we remember how our own wants can feel like needs, it can help us feel compassionate toward our children, knowing that when they say they "really need it", they really mean it.

Getting Real About Feelings

Recently, a mother told me about overhearing another mom in the park saying to her child, "I know you feel sad because your friend couldn't come over to play." She wondered what I thought about that, because it seemed to her like putting ideas in a child's head that might not be there.

I don't know if that child was sad or not. He might have been, or his mother may have been misreading something in his behavior about the way he did feel, or she might have simply been trying to console him in his disappointment about his friend. What it made me think about, though, is the way our attempts to give recognition to children's feelings sometimes sound a little rote—almost like a memorized formula. We've lost the feeling in feelings.

What I mean by that is that feelings are emotions, and are usually expressed in very emotional ways. If we are angry, or sad, or upset about something, we not only express it in words, but also in the sound of our speech, our body language, and facial expressions. We might even cry, or slam a door. The fact is there is intensity in the way the feeling is expressed. Think about it. If someone tells you they are angry in a calm, reasonable way, does that sound genuine? We often describe someone who does that as cold. Emotions are hot.

Hopefully, as adults we have some measure of control over the way we express our emotions. Children, on the other hand, are mercurial. Everything is black or white and the shift from one to the other is fluid—sometimes it seems without warning. The world—including you—is wonderful, until a dark cloud appears, and then it is terrible. Children express these feelings in extreme ways, primarily through their behavior.

118

Of course, our goal as parents is to help our children express their feelings in words. "Use your words" has almost become a mantra when children act out their emotions. But words are not that readily available to children when they are angry or upset, and even when they have them, words don't seem adequate to the feelings. We are asking them to be reasonable in the heat of emotion. Most often it is *we* they think are being unreasonable.

At the same time, almost everyone has gotten the idea that we're supposed to let children know that we recognize how they feel. Almost as often as "use your words", you can hear mothers say, "I know you are angry". Then we think that having said that in a calm, reasonable way, our children are supposed to become calm and reasonable. When they don't, we may start to feel angry that their behavior continues to be so unreasonable.

Thinking again about ourselves, if we are angry at someone for something they have done, or we think they have done, and they say in a somewhat unreal way, "I know you are angry", and then the equivalent of, "Get over it!", do we now feel better or perhaps even angrier? The point is, we want understanding and acceptance of what we are feeling.

In the same way, our children want to let us know how strongly they feel about a situation and we have to let them know in a convincing way that we do. But we can't expect that just by recognizing the feeling verbally we will make it go away. Accepting the anger of others is not easy, especially when it is coming from our children who often express emotions in behavior that is difficult to deal with.

We not only do not like their behavior, we really do not like it when children are angry at us. In fact, we often have a hard time truly accepting the whole range of our children's emotions. We would like them to be happy and even tempered all the time. Life would be so much easier if they were. Besides, too often when they are not it seems as though it is somehow our fault. Our children may think it is, and much of the time we think maybe it is.

There are ways we can be helpful if we are not focused on somehow making it all stop. If a child is angry and we know what it is about, we need to let him know directly that we know he didn't like it that . . . . whatever the situation might be. Let him tell you what he didn't like and show that you are listening. Maybe there is a way to work things out. If he is too angry, or the behavior doesn't permit it, you can let him know you understand how angry he is and when he is feeling better you will talk it over.

Thinking about what we ourselves find most helpful when we are angry or upset can really give us some good guidelines in responding to our children. Children are still learning about their emotions, and we can help them learn about these emotions not only by naming them, but by responding to them in a way that is real. Perhaps, most helpful is to reassure them that whatever they are feeling, they will feel better eventually. They really don't know that, and sometimes we forget it, too.

Reassurance That Is Real

Many more years ago than I can believe, my older son was having trouble learning to read. It was clear that he was upset about this because he was actually pretending to read. He would take an adult book out of the bookshelf, turn the pages and say, "I read that book."

We made an appointment for an evaluation by a learning specialist and now I was faced with the task of telling my son about it. I was filled with trepidation. How could I suggest that he had a problem? Wouldn't that make him feel worse about himself than he already did? Gathering my courage, at an appropriate moment I told him that I knew that reading was hard for him and that we were going to find someone who would help him learn.

I will never forget the expression on his face. He threw his arms around me and looked as if the weight of the world had been lifted from his shoulders. He was relieved that someone understood the difficulty he was having and would help him. He no longer had to pretend, and to deal with this alone.

It was our good fortune to have found Katrina deHirsch, a pioneer in the area of learning disabilities, dyslexia in particular. She said something I also have never forgotten and have repeated to many parents: "Childhood is the one time we're made to do things we're not good at." She was thinking that later on the typewriter would be a replacement for poor handwriting—and that was before any idea of the changes the computer would bring.

But the real lesson I learned was the fallacy of thinking we are somehow protecting our children by hiding, or avoiding things with which they may be struggling. When we pretend along with them that nothing is wrong, an unintended message is that this is so bad we have to hide it. Or that it is a failure that disappoints us and can't be acknowledged. In the same way, offering false reassurance in effect denies that there is a problem, confirming the opposite for a child—that the problem is too serious to talk about.

Think of it this way, if you try a new recipe and it is a disaster, does it help or make you feel worse to have the guests tell you it was delicious? Wouldn't it be of greater help if a good friend who was there told you the next day what went wrong, and how to fix it? Or if you make a mistake at work and try to cover it up instead of getting help with what you don't know, isn't it likely you will make the same mistake again, and start to feel incompetent?

We sometimes act as if children don't know that something is giving them trouble, and that talking about it will be a great blow. In fact children are only too aware when there is something they can't do that others around them seem to be doing with ease. They know something is wrong but don't know what it is. Sometimes they develop strategies to deal with what they can't do, like becoming disruptive or finding ways to avoid certain situations. This can make matters worse because then their avoidant behavior begins to seem like the problem while the real problem causing the behavior is still not addressed.

Children may find different things challenging at different stages of their development. A familiar example is the reaction some children have to birthday parties—even their own. Some children become upset, want to leave, not want mom or dad to leave, or cling to either parent without joining the activities at the party. Too often it is the clinging behavior, or not joining in that is seen as the problem rather than a child being overwhelmed by the crowd, noise, lack of structure or general rough and tumble atmosphere. The focus becomes, "Why can't my child separate?" rather than what does he find hard in this situation and how can I help.

When we talk to children in a real way, about a real situation, we accomplish a number of things. First of all, we show that we understand what he or she is experiencing. That in itself is reassuring, because children themselves often don't understand what is wrong, which is part of what makes it so upsetting to them.

More important still, if we understand, then maybe we can help them do something about a problem. It no longer seems so ominous. Besides, when we are accepting of a difficulty they are having, that means it is not terrible if it is hard to do something. Everyone finds something hard! Birthday parties are hard, and mom can stay if needed until they are no longer so overwhelming.

Whether the difficulty is one that needs special help, or just the help of a parent's support, talking about it in a real and accepting way offers reassurance that is real. And that is the first step in solving the problem.

Too Hard To Talk About

The death of a nine year old girl in a Tucson shooting had a strong emotional impact throughout the country. Mothers and fathers identified with the child's parents and were overcome by the thought of losing one's child. Children identified with the child and wondered if this could happen to them. As parents we confront two sets of emotions when we talk to our children about events as traumatic as this one.

But even matters closer to home can seem too hard to talk about. Sometimes our own emotions get in the way of recognizing or understanding our children's emotions. Children are concrete and quite literal about things, often responding in matter-of-fact ways that we may misunderstand as unfeeling or uncaring. A mother reported that her son, in talking to his grandmother about something he would do when he was older, said cheerfully, "You will be dead by then."

Another mother wondered how best to prepare her young daughter for the impending death of a family member. In answer to my question the mom said the child did not have any concept of death, had not had a pet that died, nor had it ever been discussed at home. Yet she later reported, that while driving, they passed a cemetery and the girl spontaneously said, "Oh look, a cemetery. That's where they put dead people".

Children are much more aware of what is going on around them than we think they are. Particularly in our media age children are exposed to many more things than we might wish them to be. When we think they are not aware of something, it is often because we would like them not to be—because of our own feeling that it is too difficult, or too painful. We want to spare our children the pain we ourselves are feeling, and may think the way to do that is to avoid talking about it.

At other times we may minimize the importance of an event as a way of denying its impact on a child. A young boy told me a fantastic story about his cat, which had been put to sleep. The family had many pets in the past and did not appreciate the child's attachment to this particular cat. His disjointed story was about an adventure the cat had, which ended with the cat now up in the sky. When I asked him if he thought this was really what had happened, he sadly said it wasn't. He was clearly struggling to cope with his confusion about what had happened and his feeling of loss.

We sometimes find ourselves trying to protect our children from things that are inevitably part of life. There are many kinds of losses, not only the death of a pet, but a friend moving away, a loved baby sitter leaving, even separation from mom when starting school. We wish our children did not have to experience these things, and want to protect our children from being hurt by these losses. There is also a fear that our children's emotional well-being will be damaged in some way. These worries interfere with our ability to talk to children not only about real things, but more importantly about their feelings and our own.

Real things that are often painful happen in life. Loved ones die, friendships end, we leave our parents. Even usual developmental steps involve giving up earlier pleasures, which is sometimes difficult to do. The question is not how to avoid painful things—which we can't do, anyway—it is how can we as parents help children gain the mastery and strength to deal with them. Just as we provide the nutrients children need for their bodies to grow, we need to help them develop the mental and emotional muscles they need to confront things that are painful.

These days when there seems to be a pill for everything, it's easy to get the idea that we're not supposed to be unhappy or uncomfortable about anything. Bad feelings are suspect. Yet it is a child's ability to bear unpleasant feelings, particularly sadness and anger, that will help him better confront many of life's events. A parent's willingness to help children recognize their feelings, express them appropriately, and cope with them, is a most important part of achieving such mastery.

It is by confronting difficulties and working our way through them, that we get stronger and gain confidence in our own abilities. And it is by supporting children through this process that parents help their children grow.

How Bad Is Mad?

When you were a child, did you ever get angry at your mother? I mean really mad, screaming, foot stamping, "I hate you!" mad. Everyone must have felt that way at some time growing up, but the question is whether you showed it or just felt it. And if you behaved the way you felt, what response did you get?

It's helpful to think about that now as a parent because the way children express anger is a big sore point in the way we react to their behavior. No one likes being the target of someone else's anger, especially if it is someone close to you. Their anger feels like an attack and can make you feel like attacking back.

Children's anger sometimes feels like an accusation—as if they're saying you are a bad mother. Sometimes they even say as much. A child may be angry because he couldn't have something he wanted, or do something he wanted to do. His angry behavior is his protest, but instead of it sounding like something about him, mom hears it as being about her—his behavior is her fault.

Many times the intensity of a child's reaction is not heard as a statement of how strongly he feels, but of how bad mom is. Mom may start to feel guilty and wonder if she did something that was wrong. More often, mothers feel their requests were perfectly reasonable and start to feel angry themselves at the child's attack. Mothers say all the time that they tell their children it's alright to be angry, but somehow it doesn't feel that way when children really express it. The *idea* of anger is not the same as anger that is *expressed*.

Real anger can feel scary. People even say things when angry like, "I could kill you for that". Of course we don't go around killing each other when we're angry, because we have control over our feelings. But children haven't yet developed those controls and they express anger in primitive ways like hitting, screaming or throwing things. This kind of behavior can feel threatening.

Children's loss of control can make us start to feel out of control ourselves. Because the behavior is unacceptable, we too often get focused on trying to stop it. Often this ends in an escalation of the situation. Not able to control our child's behavior, our own anger takes hold, and it sometimes seems as though we are getting down to our child's level. Our own anger can begin to seem even more dangerous than our child's, since as adults we are capable of inflicting more harm.

The problem is that because children have not yet developed inner controls, but act out their feelings, feelings and behavior seem to be one and the same. The feelings take form in behavior, and because the behavior feels threatening we label it "bad". Young children are unable to tell the difference between feelings and behavior and so begin to believe that it is the feelings that are bad.

The fact that angry feelings are joined emotionally to attacking behavior in childhood seems to color our response to anger throughout life. We were all children once, and sometimes still have trouble separating angry feelings from behavior, both in our children and in ourselves. We may still be afraid that the intensity of our feelings will be matched by the enormity of our actions. It can begin to feel unsafe not only to express anger but to feel it.

The result is that when it comes to our children, one way of avoiding their anger is to focus only on the behavior in which it is expressed. Since the behavior is "bad", it is easy to look at it simply as misbehavior, rather than as an expression of anger. It then becomes only something that needs correcting in the child, but it can be ignored as a statement about how a child is feeling toward his mother at that moment. Mom sees her child as needing to learn how to behave properly, rather than needing to learn how to express anger appropriately.

In fact, our job is to help our children learn that their feelings are acceptable, but hitting, screaming and throwing things are not. A mother can only teach this, though, if she herself feels that her child's anger is not dangerous to her and does not have to be wiped out in order for her to achieve her own goals.

To accept your child's anger and teach him to express it differently, you have to be ready to hear disagreement. You have to be able to tolerate the fact that your child doesn't like something you are doing—in fact doesn't like you at that moment. In other words, you have to risk feeling like a "bad" mother. If you can accept this you don't have to counterattack with your own anger, or give in, making you feel helpless and your child's anger seem powerful and frightening—to him and to you.

Siblings

Do you remember or have you ever heard of the Smothers Brothers? They were two brothers who had a comedy/variety show on TV in the Sixties. They had a recurring bit in which one brother said to the other, "Mother always loved you best". I often think of this line when mothers express their concerns to me about the relationship between their children.

One question mothers ask me about vey often has to do with the behavior of one sibling towards another. Usually, it is the older child's treatment of the younger child. But at times, it is also about the younger child's provocative behavior toward the older one. The older child pushes or hits the younger one "for no reason". The younger child annoys the older one when she is doing something, or takes her things.

What is interesting is that even when mothers describe "bad" behavior, they insist that the children really love each other, and that is what makes the behavior seem worse. When I ask a mother about her relationship with her own siblings, I usually hear one of two things: that the relationship was and is so close that she wants her own children to have the same experience. Or, on the other hand that she and her sister/brother had a terrible relationship, and she doesn't want that repeated. In either case, mothers seem invested in having children love each other.

In talking about sibling relationships, another feeling I have often heard expressed is parents' guilt toward the first child for having had a second. A young child I knew told me that his parents told him the reason they had his brother was because he was so wonderful they wanted another. He said he never believed them because if he was so wonderful why did they need another one! Like this little boy, parents sometimes feel that having a second child was a betrayal of the first. They worry about what they are afraid they are not doing with or for the firstborn because of the younger child. Or the opposite, that perhaps they are cheating the younger child because of their extra attention to the first.

Are these different feelings parents have connected in some way to the behavior of children towards each other? Perhaps they contribute, in part, to the upset and worry mothers have about this behavior. People talk matter-of-factly and with seeming acceptance of "sibling rivalry". But when such rivalry is actually expressed in words or actions, the parents' reaction is often as though something inexplicable is going on—something of a more serious nature.

Of course, bickering and children picking on each other is annoying. And at times we have to intervene physically to keep one child from hurting another. We would just like it to stop. But also, as with other kinds of behavior we don't like, it is helpful to think about what it means. Although the Smothers Brothers used it as a joke, the fact is that children compete to be the favored one, to get the most attention from Mom and Dad. That is what the rivalry is about.

Parents often defend themselves and want to prove how much attention they actually do give a particular child. It is understandable that one might feel indignant when a child acts up to get attention when you have just spent two hours doing something special together. But the feelings of children have little to do with reality (most of the time.) They would like you to be available 24/7—on call, as it were, if they want or think they need you. If you've just spent such a nice time together without his annoying little sister, why does it have to end?

The point is that children don't either love or hate their siblings—they do both. And they express their anger or hostile feelings through their behavior. We can help them with negative behavior only if we accept that there is nothing bad about the feeling. If we reproach or punish them for the behavior without acknowledging and accepting the feeling behind it, the message they get is that the feeling, too, is bad. Yet feelings *are* acceptable—it's the behavior that is not.

This means that it is not acceptable to hit your little brother even when you hate him. But children often need help in controlling their impulses when they are angry. If one child is having particular difficulty, he can be told that it is too hard for him to be with his brother at that time—but then he needs help from you to be taken out of the situation and become focused on something else.

It is so easy to fall into a pattern of seeing the younger child as the victim and the older one as the aggressor. If one child is comforted and the other scolded or punished, the anger and rivalry is intensified and reinforced. In fact, the younger child is not always the innocent victim. Even so, just as he may need comforting, the older child needs your understanding and help.

Your children may gang up on you at times when it serves their purposes. That's one of the advantages of having siblings. But save your breath and don't try to prove it's not true that "mother loves your brother best". That never works.

More About Siblings

Siblings don't come only in twos. Three seems always to be the more difficult number, and we have so many ideas about that middle one. The popular image seems to be of an unlucky middle child always getting lost between the oldest and the youngest. Sometimes the middle one is that lucky boy between two girls—or the other way around, lucky girl between two boys. But there is something to the idea of a middle child struggling to find his or her own identity.

We tend to forget that before the middle one was a "middle" she was the younger one of two. For a time she got the attention that goes with being the baby. But then when a new baby came, she did not move into the honored position of being the first born—that slot was already taken. Even as the second, the attention and investment is never the same as with the first. So absent the easy designation of oldest or youngest, it is a challenge for the middle one to find a way to stand out.

Mothers describe patterns of behavior that have come to seem almost classic. One picture is that of the middle child trying to emulate his older brother—often without success. Mothers say, "He wants to do everything his brother does and is constantly frustrated." But his interest in his brother may be experienced as annoying, leaving the middle one feeling rejected. His hurt feelings may then be expressed in angry behavior toward the younger sibling.

Another familiar picture is that of a child trying to boss her younger sibling in the same way as she feels bossed by her older sister. There are variations depending on the differences of age between the children, but often middle children feel as though they are in a no-win situation, literally caught in the middle. It is a challenge for parents—no less than for the children themselves—to establish a separate identity for the middle child.

Perhaps a deeper issue than the birth position of a child in the family is the feelings evoked in their parents by different children. Parents are fond of saying that they love their children equally. They say this to their children when accused of favoring one child over another in some way. But the issue is not love, it is rather the emotional reactions that are triggered in us by one child as compared to another. We talk about children pressing our buttons. Different children press different buttons.

It often seems as if there is an anger button, a worry button and an empathy button. One child always seems to get our goat in the way she acts, or what she says in response to something. Another child has us worried because he seems so different from everyone else in the family—he is more within himself while we are all outgoing. And still another child is just the opposite. She seems so familiar we have no trouble relating to her at all.

Sometimes the reason for our reactions seems clear: "She torments me exactly the way my sister used to when we were growing up." "My brother was like that and he ended up a real loner, not very happy." "She is just like I was at that age and I understand her perfectly." Here we are at least somewhat aware that we are identifying a child with someone else of significance in our lives.

But at other times the reasons for our reactions are more elusive and seem harder to get a handle on. When that happens, the child in question can begin to seem like more of a problem. When we are not aware of what we are bringing to the situation we start to attribute more to the child. This is not to say that a child's behavior may not be an issue. But rather we become handicapped in our own responses if we are reacting to someone or something else in our lives, past or present, rather than to this child at this moment.

It is truly a challenge to see and relate to each child as an individual in his or her own right, whatever the position in the family. Mothers sometimes tell me they have trouble with a child's personality or behavior because it is so unlike her other children. She has a different picture in her mind of how children react, or are supposed to react in certain situations.

But differences in themselves don't mean bad, good or something wrong. We have to remind ourselves to look at behavior in terms of what we can understand about each child's own personality and feelings, not in terms of someone else. In particular, we have to be mindful that our children are not extensions of ourselves. They have a right to be who they are. Our job is to get to know who each of them is.

About Parents

Doctor, Lawyer, Indian Chief

A well known psychiatrist who studied children said that you could see the differences in babies' personalities at birth just by observing them in a nursery. (Of course that was in the days before mothers and babies were sent home before they could even catch their breath.) He talked about the "executive baby", who already seemed to be bossing everyone around, the "demanding baby", who managed to get more attention than others, the "winning baby", whom everyone immediately loved, among other examples.

Mothers also have definite ideas about what their children were like as babies and will describe them as easy, difficult, active, having a mind of their own and so on. Do such descriptions match up in any way to their personalities as they develop? A friend wrote to me in response to my last article saying she wasn't sure we really understand our children's personalities when they are young. She wondered if that is why we read so much of ourselves or our own histories in them.

Actually, there are many reasons that we find it challenging to see our children as their own people separate from ourselves. The fact that mothers carry babies in their bodies begins a very strong connection. We imagine even before birth what the baby will be like. Sometimes it's hard to shift from the imagined baby to the real baby, since they are rarely the same.

Of course there are genetic connections as well. Children look like this or that member of the family. They may have similar personality characteristics or behavioral traits. Even as development progresses, your mother or mother-in-law may say that you or your husband were just like that. It's easy to get mixed up and think that you and your child are the same person. On the other hand, if we expect that kind of identification and instead a child seems very different, that can become a cause for concern, or of feeling disconnected from one's child.

We ourselves may have childhood memories of not having felt understood by our parents. We may even have felt they wanted things for us that were not what we wanted for ourselves. Sometimes as parents we set about trying to correct whatever we didn't like in our own growing up. In trying to do that, without realizing it we may repeat the same thing our parents did—namely treating our children as though they are us, fixing our own lives through our children. Or realizing our own ambitions through our children.

What makes it difficult to separate our children from ourselves is that not only do we want the best for our children, but we are responsible for them for many years. Someone once said that children are entitled to make their own mistakes, just as we did. There is much wisdom in that, but it is understandable that as parents we want our children to learn from our experience, to try to keep them from the mistakes we think they are making or about to make.

It is often hard to know when children need to be protected from their own behavior and when to leave them alone to learn from their own mistakes. We don't try to stop children from walking because they fall down while learning. We pick them up and help them keep going. On the other hand, we do intervene if they are trying to climb way beyond their ability and are likely really to get hurt. It can be hard at times, to make a judgment about which is which.

Perhaps what is most challenging is not so much understanding the personalities of our children when they are young, but recognizing their behavior when it is consistent with who they are. A good example is children who are cautious in social situations. A mother may aptly describe such a child as "slow to warm up". Yet the behavior itself becomes a cause for concern, at times because mom herself was like that and feels it was a handicap. She wants to correct in her child a part of her temperament or personality and has trouble accepting who her child is, rather than who she wants her to be—or not to be.

The same is true for other behavior, such as when children are self-assertive, willful, observers more than participants, or loners rather than joiners. Because children are still learning how to function in the world they may not always moderate their behavior in ways that serve them well in various situations. As when they were learning to walk, we now need to help them achieve their goals without trying to change who they are.

An old song says "neither doctor, lawyer, nor Indian chief could love you any more than I do." Perhaps it should be, "whether you're a doctor, lawyer or Indian Chief, I couldn't love you more than I do."

Ghosts

Halloween has long since gone, hopefully taking all the goblins and other scary things with it. Sometimes, though, it seems as if there are still some ghosts hanging around. Children often think they see them in their room at night when they are fighting sleep. But parents also may find them in some dark corners of the house.

Many of you perhaps have read a wonderful book called "The Magic Years" by Selma Fraiberg, a psychoanalyst who worked with parents and children. Her book offers great understanding of children's minds when they are very young. She also wrote about something she called "Ghosts in the Nursery", which had more to do with parents.

The "ghosts in the nursery" are things we experienced when we ourselves were children, which sometimes pop up to haunt us when we become parents. Those ghosts may have to do with relationships we had with our own parents, or things about ourselves that may have caused us difficulty. Without realizing it, those old ghosts can influence the way we see our own children and the way we interact with them.

Often these ghosts turn up when something in a child's behavior or development concerns us. Many times when a child is especially active, or rebellious, or otherwise difficult to handle, a mother will say, "My mother says I was just like that. Now I can understand what she went through". Or "My mother-in-law says my husband was the same way—and he still is!"

We're used to those comparisons made about physical traits: he has his father's eyes, she has her mother's hair. Children usually grow up hearing them—more than once. But seeing a child's behavior or personality traits through the lens of the parents' childhood can interfere with our ability to know who our child really is himself or herself. Seeing certain things in our child that we identify with ourselves at times makes us feel proud. On the other hand, if it is something we don't like about ourselves—or our mate—it can lead us to misread its significance for the child, and to respond in negative ways.

Sometimes we want our children to make up for things that were missing or that we regret about our own childhood. One father was determined to have his son excel at sports because his own lack of skill in this area had led to his feelings of exclusion. Sports were not a source of interest or ability for his son, and the father's insistence on his son improving his skills were actually producing in the boy the same kind of feelings the father had growing up.

Relationships with other family members can also play a role. A mother talked to me about the difficulties she was having with a daughter who seemed very needy and demanding of her attention. The mom identified her with her own sister who was very demanding, got all of their mother's attention, and who had many difficulties later on when they were grown. She did not want this to happen to her daughter and responded punitively to the child's behavior.

In fact, this was a middle child who was very sensitive and immature in some areas. She had some real difficulties with separation, which were being intensified by what she experienced as her mother's rejecting behavior. When this mother realized that she was responding to her child as if she were her sister, she also saw that she was trying to correct what she thought were her own mother's failures. Once becoming aware of this, she was able to appreciate that her daughter had some real needs which she could respond to in more appropriate ways.

When parents to be are expecting a child, part of pregnancy is imagining what that expected child will be like. A connection is made with that imagined child. When the real baby arrives, part of the challenge for parents is dealing with the difference between the real and the imagined child. And that challenge recurs at various times as a child grows and develops.

Our imagined children are always perfect. Our real children never are. The "ghosts" may make their appearance when we react to what we may see as our children's "imperfections". Of course our own upbringing plays a big role in how we raise our children. But in thinking about our own lives, it helps to recognize that our children are entitled to their own. You are not your mother or father and your child is not you. Her life will be different from yours.

Ghosts are often invisible. Bringing them into view is what makes it possible to sweep them away.

All I Need To Know

"All I really need to know about how to live and what to do and how to be I learned in Kindergarten." This is an often quoted line from a book by Robert Fulghum in which he identifies some early lessons learned and points out how they could—or should—be applied to adult life.

Some of the lessons mentioned, "share everything, play fair, don't hit people, put things back where you found them, don't take things that aren't yours", have a familiar ring. Parents are trying to teach those things even before kindergarten, although they loom larger when children are learning to function with others in a group.

The idea in Fulghum's book is to show how the things children learn when they are young we need to carry over to the way we live in the world as grown-ups. Actually, I have found that it works the other way around. If we look at the way we live together as adults, the things that are important to us, the things that bother us, the conflicts that arise and the way we do or don't resolve them, we can discover a lot about teaching our children "how to live and what to do and how to be."

The problem is that many of these lessons go against strong feelings that we struggle with. For example, "share everything". Do you really want to share everything? Don't you have some things you don't want your children to play with, or something you would prefer that someone else not borrow? Children, too, have prize possessions that they don't want to share with a friend or sibling. So "share everything" is too simple and may be unfair to expect of our children.

How about "play fair"? Isn't the game more fun when you win? Have you ever had the impulse to cheat? What helps you overcome it—if you do? Knowing that it is "wrong" is only the first part. Young children don't yet have the concept, but even when they get it, they still have to overcome the strong wish to win that most of us have.

Then there is "don't hit people". That seems obvious. No one wants to be hit back. But how about feeling so angry about something someone does that you would like to sock them. And haven't we all had the feeling now and then of wanting to give our children a good slap? As with the impulse to cheat, we sometimes have to work hard not to act on those feelings.

"Put things back where you found them." If only! Are you a put-awayer or a leaver-outer? How about your mate or partner? Is one person messy and the other a neat freak? That can cause some friction when people live together. So what do we do when children don't put their toys away?

"Don't take things that aren't yours." Women sometimes complain about sisters who "borrowed" their clothes. Children sometimes "borrow" things from school or from a brother or sister. They often "take" things that another child was playing with. Is that taking things that aren't yours?

The point about all these rules and instructions we're always giving children is that in adult life we still struggle with many or most of them. The reason is that what seem like basic, simple things are often really quite difficult. They go against what feels like our own self-interest, or whatever we would most like to do at the moment.

From another vantage point, following these "rules" and going against what we want at the moment is really *in* our self-interest. We are all social animals and the ability to live together more, rather than less pleasurably is definitely very much to our self-interest. And guidelines on how to live and what to do remind us that others also have needs and feelings to be considered.

It takes time and effort to help children understand the underlying reason for all the do's and don'ts. The meaning of some of this thinking will take a while for them to be able to grasp. Neither is it helpful to get involved in long explanations for everything we ask them to do or not do. So we use "do" and "don't" as short cuts, basically asking children to just do what we ask of them.

Becoming aware of how we ourselves are handling these do's and don'ts can help us really understand what it is our children have to master in themselves. It can enable us to be more compassionate in the way we give corrections to our children while they work to overcome the impulses we may still be struggling with. It can also help us be less judgmental of behavior that is all too human.

Perhaps the truth is that everything we need to know we started to learn in Kindergarten—and are still learning.

A Dad Moment

School's out, so I often see children on the bus these days with a mom or dad, sometimes a baby-sitter, or even a grandparent. This week it was a dad with two boys and a baby, who came on and sat down right across from me. The boys were about seven and four, the younger one wearing a helmet, the older boy carrying his. They both had leg and knee pads on and obviously were returning from some sports activity. They looked it, too, all hot and sweaty.

Dad was a really big, tall guy wearing a squashy Australian kangaroo hat. He was "wearing" the baby on his shoulder, but once he sat down he held the baby in a rocking position without any rocking. At first the baby looked like a newborn—maybe in contrast to the big father. With what followed it became clear this was not a newborn, but a three month old at most.

The baby (never could determine the sex) was quiet at first, but then began to fuss. Dad moved him/her around a bit, including back over his shoulder. This did not soothe the fussing, which then turned into real crying. Dad now put the baby stomach down on his extended, open hand and began doing airplane swooping motions back and forth. He made pretend swoops to the older boy who was sitting next to him, and who made contact with the baby each time. The father had a long reach, so the baby on his hand was well out away from his body. (The baby's ability to hold its head without support told me it was not a newborn.)

I have to confess that my heart was in my mouth as I watched this, and it took enormous self-restraint just to sit quietly by. What I was thinking, though, was that if the mother of this baby had seen this she might have had an anxiety attack. The baby, on the other hand, stopped crying and seemed pleased with the experience. There was more to come, as the older boy wanted to hold the baby on his lap, Dad placed the baby on the boy's lap, though thankfully did keep a watchful hand close by. The baby was now the picture of contentment, although the older brother soon tired of being in charge and the baby was returned to the father's care.

During this whole scene, the father stayed in touch with his other two children, responding to their comments or questions. When it was time to get off, they all stood up and marched out in a line—baby back on Dad's shoulder. As they passed by me I couldn't resist, and leaning forward I said to the father, "You are a great Dad!" I was rewarded with a grin from ear to ear.

This was really a teaching moment and a learning moment for me. Of course I knew that moms and dads play with children and care for them differently. In a previous article I even wrote about fathers being more physical in their play with children. But seeing this Dad's apparent self-confidence in his unusual and creative way of comforting this very young and small baby was a real eye-opener (in more ways than one!)

I certainly don't mean that all fathers should, or would even want to turn their little babies into airplanes. But what I found myself thinking about was the somewhat limited way in which we tend to define nurturing. Perhaps because historically and traditionally women have cared for children, we think of nurture in terms of softness, breasts, gentleness and a certain kind of protectiveness. We tend to put upset babies up against our bodies and pat their backs and use a soothing voice to comfort them, not fly them through the air.

In fairness to other dads it's important to note that this baby was the third child, with two older brothers who looked pretty physical themselves, so this dad had already had plenty of experience. That lucky third child gets the benefit of all that experience and the dad's accrued confidence. But fathers generally should be supported in their own ways of caring for children and in using their initiative to deal with upsets.

My word to moms, including myself, is that children are a lot more resilient than we think. They also enjoy ways of being handled that seem off the charts. They won't break, and probably will even develop their own self-confidence in the process.

The best part of the experience was the Dad's obvious pleasure at my comment. Both fathers and mothers need that pat on the back—they get enough criticism. Let's remember to offer one—a pat, not a criticism—whenever we can. In fact, let's start a Praise A Parent Campaign.

Praise A Parent

During our Praise A Parent Campaign, I have been noticing and thinking about all the things that are part of a mother's job description. Often people think a mother's job is simply the physical care of children. But that's the easy part.

A child's development, which so often seems just to happen, is actually the result of a teaching and learning process. Mothers themselves sometimes don't seem to realize when they are teaching and how much they are teaching. Child rearing is really education. A child must learn the skills he needs to function independently and the behavior that will help him become a social being. And usually his mother is his first teacher.

Mothers teach children to drink from a cup, to eat with a spoon and fork, to dress themselves, to use the toilet. They teach children to put away their toys, to share, not to hit or bite, to respect the rights of others. They help children develop the skills they need, and teach them acceptable behavior.

This teaching and learning take place in many different ways—some that we don't even think about. Children learn a lot by watching us—which we often don't even realize until we see them imitating our behavior, or hear our words coming back to us. They learn through repetition—how many times have you had to read the same story? They learn through trial and error. They learn by watching, listening, doing. They learn through experiences that are pleasurable (and at times not so pleasurable), and not beyond their capabilities.

So, to be successful we have to match the way we are teaching to what a child is physically, emotionally, and intellectually capable of learning. Obviously, you wouldn't use complicated verbal instructions with a child who is just beginning to use language. You wouldn't try to teach her to tie her shoelaces if she didn't yet have the fine motor coordination that would enable her to succeed. Other kinds of teaching and learning are not as clear cut.

How do mothers learn how to do this? Largely they learn from their observation and understanding of their own children. A mother learns such things as how long her child is able to concentrate on a task, how much help he is likely to need to accomplish a task she has in mind, how much self-control he is capable of, what kinds of situations are particularly frustrating to him. If mom is off base, her child's reactions and behavior let her know that soon enough. A mother learns from her child what she needs to know in order most effectively to help him learn from her. It's kind of a reciprocal learning process.

Mothers come to see me when they get stuck in this process. Why do they get stuck? At times this happens when children respond or behave in ways that you don't expect. Or in ways that you don't like. That's when thoughts start to go in the direction of "what's wrong?" "Is this normal?" But mothers almost always know the answers to their own questions.

I have found that mothers often don't know how much they know. They certainly know their own children better than anyone else. Whenever I ask a mother why she thinks her child is behaving in a particular way she almost always knows the answer. She just doesn't believe she knows the answer. I often ask a mother, if your child could tell you in words what he is saying through his behavior, what would he say? Bingo! Moms almost always can tell me. Once you know what your child is telling you, it's not that hard to figure out what to do about it.

The fact that mothers know their children as well as they do enables them to be good teachers. Since starting the Praise A Parent Campaign I have seen moms teaching in so many ways.

The mom I saw who was explaining to her little one why steam was coming out of a building vent. The mom who was helping her child become less irritable by finding the pleasure in a social exchange. The mom in the park who was doing conflict resolution when two kids each wanted to play the game his way. The mom I overheard helping her daughter feel less anxious about a camp activity.

These are some of the things we frequently take for granted that we need instead to notice and praise. We are the ones who can let other mothers know they are doing a good job.

Praise a parent today!

Parent Values

There have been some interesting comments by readers in response to the articles posted as part of our Praise A Parent Campaign. There was one a number of weeks ago that I would like to comment on. This reader refers to going to a public pool in her neighborhood and writes, "On occasion I see a parent who speaks in a friendly, respectful tone, explains to her child, for example, when they will have to leave and why, and gives regular updates as to how much time is left. Though clearly in charge, she isn't heavy handed, does not resort to bribes, threats, etc. When I witness this I feel like complimenting the parent . . . ."

It struck me that both parents involved, the observer and the one observed, are reflecting a set of values about parent-child relationships. So often parents ask for the "right" way to handle this or that issue with a child. The idea seems to be that the right techniques will avoid conflict and solve problems—that there is a "right" way to raise children. Yet so much of the way we respond to our children is actually an expression of our own personal values about relationships generally, and with children in particular.

Let's look at the values involved in the comment I have quoted. The first, and perhaps most fundamental, is the "friendly, respectful tone". I don't think the writer means the mother is talking to her child as a friend, but rather that she is not using a critical or bossy voice. The word "respectful" is most significant. To me this means the mother sees her child as another person with feelings and wishes, who deserves to be considered. This is further elaborated on in "explains to her child when they will have to leave and why." This decision is based in reality, which she shares with her child, rather than on an arbitrary whim of mom's.

"She gives regular updates as to how much time is left." Here too, the mother is respecting the fact that children have a poor concept of time, and have difficulty moving from one activity to another—especially when it entails leaving something they like. Updates about time left helps keep a child on track.

"Though clearly in charge, she isn't heavy handed." In a way, that is the most difficult thing to accomplish. Often "heavy handed" means acting bossy, which in turn can come from *not* feeling in charge. Conveying the sense of being in charge really does come from feeling in charge, from feeling confident about what you are asking or doing. Without that feeling of confidence, too often a parent can end up sounding as though she is either giving an order or asking for a child's o.k.

"Does not resort to bribes, threats, etc." Bribes reflect a parent's belief that a child will not respect her request—that it will not be valid enough in and of itself for her child to comply. Threats imply an attempt at coercion to bring about a desired result. Both suggest an absence of mutual respect between parent and child.

Perhaps the most important thing about this anecdote is that it describes what must be the kind of ongoing relationship that exists between a mother and child. Treating each other with respect is not a one time event. To have a meaningful impact on behavior, a climate of mutual respect has to be established over time. Children trust that they will be considered, while parents understand that children are still learning to consider others—their parents first of all.

Even when parents value treating others with respect, this often doesn't get carried over to relationships with their children. Part of the reason for this is a hangover of an older set of values that said children should be seen and not heard. The feeling still lingers that children should just do as they are told—that the wishes of the adult are inherently more important than those of the child.

Too often the idea of respecting a child's feelings and wishes gets translated as doing whatever a child wants. But what it really means is respecting the fact that a child's feelings and wishes are as important to a child as the parent's wishes are to her—or him. Actually, this is part of making all relationships work—recognizing what is important to another person as well as what is important to oneself.

It is giving this recognition to a child that helps him learn to accept not always getting what he wants. A parent respecting a child's wishes, showing they are being considered, is an important part of teaching him to respect the wishes of others—especially the parent.

Do As I Do

Parents sometimes joke about telling children to "Do as I say, not as I do". When we say that it's because we inwardly admit to ourselves that we are not always a model for the way we want our children to behave.

This was brought home to me by a talk a Swedish doctor gave on kindness, which a friend called to my attention. The talk itself was interesting in that the speaker makes the point that kindness to others is not just a noble virtue, it is also in our own self-interest to behave that way. One reason he gives as an example, is that our own behavior influences others. If we treat others with kindness they are apt to treat us the same way.

In the talk he gives a demonstration of the power of imitation. He performs a kind of "Simon says" exercise, telling the audience they are to do whatever he says. While telling them what to do he demonstrates: touch your nose, touch your head, touch your chest, touch your mouth. But this time when he says touch your mouth he puts his own hand to his ear. Only one person in the audience followed the instruction to touch his mouth. All the others did what the doctor did, not what he said, and touched their ears.

This is a very dramatic demonstration of the power of imitation. But those of us who are parents are all too aware of the role of imitation in children's learning. Often we think about it in connection with children learning things we don't like from others. Have you ever said, or heard others say, "He learned those words from the kids in school". Or, "She picked that up from the child next door." We worry about what our children are learning from what they see on television or in the movies.

But how about the things they learn by imitating us? Imitation is part of most learning, beginning early on. See how intently a baby studies your face when you babble and coo at her. Children copy the names we give to things, watch the way we do many things, such as learning to eat with utensils, manipulate objects, even turning on the remote control to the tv.

They also learn things we may not be aware we are teaching them. Have you ever asked a family member to tell someone on the phone you are not in because you don't want to talk to her? Have you ever written a note to school saying your child was home with a cold when in reality a conflicting family plan had been made? Have you ever told someone her outfit was beautiful when you thought it most unattractive?

Little white lies seem to be part of what makes the world go around, avoiding hurting people's feelings and at times smoothing difficult situations for ourselves. But our children are also getting the message that this is the way to handle things—and they don't always apply what they see in ways of which we approve. Children often skirt the truth as a way to avoid parental disapproval or anger.

"Did you take your brother's toy?" "No, he lost it." Or, "Who turned the tv on?" "I didn't do it!" Children are at times accused of lying in such situations and are strongly disapproved of. We criticize them for telling untruths to avoid blame or punishment. Yet it is not clear to them how this differs from some of the things they have seen us do, or the way we have handled certain situations.

We learn in life that it would not always be helpful or useful to be completely honest with everyone about everything. Everything is not black or white, and part of maturity is learning to respond appropriately depending on the circumstances. Children are more concrete, and do tend to see things as black or white-shades of grey are more elusive. One way we can help them learn is to become clearer ourselves about what we are doing and the ways in which our children may be imitating us.

This happens on so many levels, not just the little white lies, but the way we respond to a request for a favor from a friend or the beggar on the street, from the things we choose to buy or not buy, even the general way we interact with others—those we know as well as those we don't.

Whether we like it or not, too often the real message our children take from us is, "Do as I do, not as I say". That is the message children get—even when we don't realize we are delivering it.

Ask Dr. Mom

Years ago I consulted a doctor about my child's confusing medical problem. He asked me a lot of questions and my answers helped solve the problem. I told him that no one ever asked me those questions before and he said that in medical school a pediatrics professor taught him, "If you don't know what's wrong with a child, ask the mother."

I have been following that advice in my own work with mothers and have found that it is absolutely true. When mothers ask me what is causing a child's behavior that is worrying them, they usually know the answer themselves. They know the answer because they have understood the child's behavior. Their seeming confusion comes in part from not having enough confidence in their own answer. But it may also come from not liking the answer.

Children communicate through behavior. Actually, we all do. As adults we have a greater mastery of language—and hopefully of our feelings—which enables us to communicate to others more clearly and directly. Not always, though. If a friend responds in a snappy way, we might wonder if something we said annoyed her. If a spouse blows up seemingly for no reason, we might think something must have happened at work, or wonder if we did something to cause the behavior, or just feel angry at the outburst.

So everyone communicates through behavior as well as words; we interpret the behavior, and our interpretations influence our response. The same is true of our interactions with our children. If a child becomes angry and defiant, or unusually quiet and withdrawn, we try to figure out what that behavior means. The problem comes when our own reaction to the behavior interferes with our ability to understand it.

Angry and defiant behavior is very unpleasant, so the focus becomes the behavior itself—what to do about the behavior. But how can you know what to do about the behavior if you haven't stopped to understand what it—or your child—is telling you? That's when our thoughts start to turn to discipline, or punishment for the behavior.

On the other hand, if I ask a mother, "What do you think he is so angry about?" mom will tell me he resents all the attention his sister has been getting, or he is angry at her for restricting his watching television. In the same way, the mother of a withdrawn child might tell me her daughter feels excluded by some of the girls at school, or that she may be reacting to too many after school activities.

In both instances our emotional response to the behavior gets in our way. A child's angry or defiant behavior often makes us angry in turn. Withdrawn or unhappy-seeming behavior can cause us to worry that something is wrong. To the degree that we're angry or worried, it seems that the behavior must have some special meaning that is beyond our grasp. We may start to label the behavior as "bad", or "not normal", and look for methods that will fix it.

A child's behavior, (adults' behavior, too, if you think about it,) has two parts. One part is the communication, and the other part is the means of delivery. I think of that as the medium and the message: the medium is the behavior and the message is the content to be communicated. We often don't like the behavior—the method of communication—and so forget to think about the message itself.

But sometimes we also don't like the message. We don't like it if a child is angry at us. We don't like to know that something is making our child unhappy. We may not like hearing it, but hearing the message can tell us how to begin to respond to it. The behavior is an expression of how strongly a child feels about something, but the message tells us what he feels so strongly about. We have to address both the message and the feelings. If we want to correct the method of delivery (the behavior), we have to first show that we heard the message.

Letting a child know that we understand what he is angry about is a good first step. We can then also think about why the child was *so* angry. Usually this entails a conflict of wishes between mother and child, and perhaps there is a better way to resolve whatever the conflict was about. That doesn't mean things will go the way the child wanted. It does mean showing your child a willingness to understand his feelings and listen to his point of view.

In the same way, our worry about the child who seems withdrawn or unhappy, can be turned instead into an acknowledgement of what is going on that she may have felt unable to share. Here, too, the support offered for a child's feelings can go a long way in beginning to address the problem.

The point is not to turn away from your own understanding of what your child's behavior is about—whatever the behavior is. The behavior persists when the child feels not heard. The same is true for us as adults, too. We all want to feel understood, even when we can't have what we want.

What About Fathers?

Yes, what about fathers! We expect a lot more of fathers than we used to. They are also getting more scrutiny as a result—to which mothers have long been exposed. Actually, some of that scrutiny comes from mothers themselves, who are used to playing the major role in child-rearing (and certainly child care.)

Despite their own anxieties, mothers—and often fathers agree—consider themselves the greater authority about their children. Starting in infancy mothers and babies seem to have a special bond, especially if moms are nursing. Although dads have learned how to do bottle feeding and change diapers, the baby's seeming preference for mom can make dads feel shut out.

Feeling this way can lead fathers to try to do things the way mom does it. And trying to imitate someone else can be very inhibiting. One father said he felt incompetent when caring for his son until he became aware that he was trying to follow exactly what his wife did. Once he realized this, he decided to do whatever came more naturally to him, and things were much better after that.

Fathers and mothers are also men and women . . . . who are known often to approach things differently. Fathers play with children differently than mothers do. They are more inclined toward physical activity and their interactions with their children are likely to take that form. They can often tolerate or even encourage more daring behavior, such as climbing higher on the jungle gym in the playground. Mothers sometimes complain about fathers over-stimulating children by roughhousing with them before bedtime. Fathers, on the other hand, may complain that mothers are "too soft", and give in to children too easily.

Sometimes fathers feel strongly about authority and react if they feel challenged by a child. One father punished his son for calling him names. Mom, on the other hand, understood that the boy was angry at his father for making him take his construction apart in order to put it away. It seems not unusual for mothers and fathers to disagree about punishment, with Mom feeling that Dad is taking too hard a line. Of course, sometimes the opposite is true; mothers may feel that fathers undermine *their* authority.

Mothers and fathers may each unwittingly reinforce the very positions they oppose in their mates. Mom tries to compensate for Dad's toughness by becoming more indulgent, which in turn, causes Dad to become tougher to make up for Mom's indulgence. Children can be very adept at using this phenomenon to play parents off against each other to their own advantage: telling Mom, "Dad says it's o.k.", and to Dad, "Mom said I can do it." When mothers and fathers are able to be responsive to each other's point of view, however, the approach of each may be modified, and children can then benefit from these differences in their parents.

One important gender difference that can interfere with the ability of parents to solve parenting questions is that men tend to be invested in fixing problems, while women are often more focused on understanding feelings. This sometimes plays out as action vs. empathy . . . and conflict between parents. In the earlier example of the boy and his construction, to Dad it was more important to *do* something about the behavior, while Mom wanted Dad to *understand* why the child was angry at him. Although they both agreed that the behavior was not acceptable, they ended up being angry at each other.

The thing to remember is that differences in approach do not mean that one person is right and the other wrong. Mothers and fathers each have something important to contribute. It is as important for parents to be able to "hear" each other as it is for both to "hear" their children. "Hearing" means listening. It doesn't mean you have to do what the other person says. It does mean taking the other's point of view into consideration, whether it is your spouse or your child. This kind of listening can often lead to a solution both parents can support, which in turn will make it a better solution both for the problem and for the child.

Fathers are learning how to be fathers—not mothers. Everyone learns best when praised for things done well, rather than criticized for doing it the "wrong way". Fathers and mothers each need the support and approval of the other, just as children do from both parents.

Please and Thank-You

In an ice-cream shop recently, a mom and dad with their little boy were about to be served. The child looked about two, or two and a half, and his dad picked him up so he could see the flavors and talk to the man waiting to help him. In a very grown-up voice the child said, "I'd like an ice-cream cone please." It was quite endearing, and the server was happy to help him. As I was leaving I told the mom that I liked the way her little boy said "please". She smiled with pleasure and said, "We try".

I was impressed with the natural way in which the little boy said "please", without any prompting. I hear mothers working on "please and thank-you" all the time. Sometimes a request is not granted until the child says "please". A favorite reminder is, "What's the magic word?" At other times it is a somewhat critical, "You forgot something." Children react in ways that indicate this is a familiar refrain—either with annoyance or slight embarrassment—as they make the needed correction.

Parents are often not only concerned about "please" and "thank you", but shaking hands when introduced to someone, eating with the proper utensils, or even responding when asked a question. In general, many parents are focused on teaching children manners, and wonder when it is realistic to begin teaching and expecting certain behavior along these lines.

When children don't have "good manners"—or when they do—mothers often feel that this reflects well or poorly on them. The mother in the ice-cream shop certainly accepted my praise of her son as praise for her. Her response, "We try", says that her son's behavior is a product of the parents' teaching.

What are good manners and why are they important? Too often we forget to answer that question to ourselves. We lose the meaning of what we really want to teach, and end up simply trying to train our children in a kind of rote behavior. When that happens, children respond as if this is just one more annoying adult demand. They may comply or shake it off, but either way it has no significant meaning to them.

Manners are forms of behavior, some of which are more important to some people than to others. Manners may show consideration of others, or at times respect for others, or in some instances simply make human interaction go more smoothly. If you say "I'm sorry", to someone you accidently bump into on the bus, you let them know you did not intentionally hurt them and regret the incident. "Please" can differentiate a request from a demand, while "Thank-you" expresses appreciation.

The other day it was pouring rain, the bus was crowded and people were dealing with wet umbrellas, needing to pass others as they got on and off. A little girl of about four or five was sitting next to her mom who was preoccupied with her phone. The girl had a balloon which she was pushing back and forth toward people standing in front of her, and rubbing it with her hand to make a most unpleasant noise. It seemed clear she wanted her mother's attention but in the meantime was annoying everyone around her. Finally, the mom herself was annoyed and angrily told her daughter to stop, going right back to her phone messages.

One could say the child had "bad manners", but the most striking thing was her indifference to, and lack of awareness of, the impact of her behavior on others. Here is a situation where the reprimand for her behavior addressed nothing else—not the impact of this behavior on others, or the inappropriate way of seeking attention. In this instance, mom's behavior showed the same lack of awareness as her daughter's. Her "manners" were also missing.

The point is that the surface behavior we call "manners" can have real meaning when it speaks to something important in human relationships. If we focus solely on teaching our children correct forms, and leave out the substance—the meaning and purpose of the behavior—then children have no real understanding of what they are supposed to learn. It is like learning the words of a story without knowing what the story is about.

As with so much else in our children's development, they learn about manners from us. They imitate us and identify with us. We teach them through our own behavior towards each other—but also toward them. We don't like it when they make demands, or interrupt us, or are inconsiderate. But without realizing it, we may be doing the same thing to them. It's just possible that more "pleases" from us will bring "thank-you" more often from them.

True Grit

There has been much focus recently on testing and raising scores as a measure of children's academic progress. But there are some educators who are more interested in understanding what it is that really helps children succeed, both in school and in life. The New York Times reported on one such inquiry into what qualities are most predictive of that kind of success.

The investigators in this study found that the quality most significant in outstanding achievement was determination and persistence in working toward a goal no matter what the obstacles or what the length of time it would take. The name given to that particular quality was "grit", and the challenge for educators became how to instill that quality in students.

Reading this report made me think about articles I posted recently which pointed to children not making the connection between input and outcome. Too often there is an expectation that things should come easily, and then the feeling that something is wrong—either with them or with what is expected of them—when things don't. Children often don't accept the fact that real work may have to go into achieving their goals.

The newspaper article's headline was, "What if the Secret to Success Is Failure?" The idea seemed to be that failure builds persistence, or "grit". This seems to me, to be misleading and not particularly useful. The thinking behind this is that surviving failure leads to the ability to overcome obstacles in achieving one's goals. But how does one learn to overcome failure in the first place?

Undoubtedly, there are a number of factors that contribute to such an ability. One is certainly resilience. There are some children who just seem able to bounce back more readily from disappointments. Others who seem undaunted when met by obstacles in getting what they want. But at the other end of the spectrum are children who seem by nature not to be fighters and who accept defeat more readily.

The question for parents, however, is whether there is anything in our own interactions with our children that can help them develop persistence in the face of obstacles? This question goes back to one that parents think about from our children's earliest years. It has to do with finding the right balance between frustration and gratification in responding to our children's needs and wishes.

Somehow the idea has taken hold—perhaps through misinterpretations of psychological theories—that frustration is bad. The thought is that frustration is damaging to children's development and can lead to a lack of self-confidence and a poor self-image. On another level, we don't like having to deal with children's behavior when they are frustrated.

The other side of the picture is that we all like to gratify our children. It makes us feel good to be able to give children what they want and need—not to mention that they are then also so much easier to handle and more pleasurable to be with. This has become part of feeling like a "good mother".

But the point is that frustration is an inevitable and necessary part of life. Things happen in life over which we have no control, and our goal is to have our children develop the strength to deal with them if and when they happen. Of course, our hope is that they will not have to deal with things that are beyond their age and capacity. But neither does it help to try to protect them from the usual, unavoidable frustrations of everyday life.

This issue comes up daily in the most ordinary, commonplace ways. A child wants a cookie when it's just before lunch time. Or she wants ice-cream on the way home from school that you don't think she should have. Or he must have that toy he saw on television. So often the temptation is just to give in to avoid a confrontation, or a tantrum, or other unpleasantness. On the other hand, one's thinking is sometimes, why not? It's harmless and makes the child happy.

The point is not to allow the child to be frustrated for the sake of some hypothetical benefit of frustration. Rather, the reality is that we can't have everything we want in life and that is a hard lesson for children to learn and for us as parents to teach. Children can learn from these small frustrations and disappointments that it is possible to survive them. They discover their own ability to master such experiences and move on. These are the building blocks that ultimately enable them to overcome more difficult obstacles.

Our own "grit" as parents may lie in helping children live through the tantrums or other reactions to frustration and disappointment, as unpleasant as that may be for us, so that they can experience that sense of mastery.

"True grit" may actually begin when you find you are able to wait until after lunch to get that cookie.

Using Judgment

In many of the issues I've written about there is a recurring theme that parents should use their judgment in making decisions about their children. This comes up especially in relation to research findings that seem to advise parents, or at least lead to a conclusion, about what is best for children.

I urge parents to rely on their own judgment in many matters because all children are different, are at different stages of development, and parents are the ones who best know their own child. Yet, I know parents often feel that there is a decision that is *really* right that should be made about something that concerns them about their children, and that is the answer they are looking for. The temptation is to look to some "expert" to give it to them.

Mothers often ask me such questions as, Is it time to move my child from a crib to a bed? Is it bad if my child comes into my bed at night? My child cries when I leave her at school, should I be staying there with her? My child protests that he doesn't want to go to school, should I let him stay home? My child won't join in group activities, should he be allowed just to watch?

These are not easy questions, and most of the time the answer seems to begin with, "it depends . . . .". The point is, it may be easier to say use your judgment than to make that judgment. It is not surprising that we wish someone would give us the "right" answer, so we could be certain we are making the "right" decision. We don't always trust that we really do know what is best for our own child.

One reason it is not easy to feel confident about our own judgment is that there are usually so many factors involved. For example, a child resisting going to school raises a number of questions. Once children are of legal school age, going to school is not a choice, so that is one kind of issue.

On the other hand, one mother I know was torn about the upset her nursery school age child was having about leaving for school because as she pointed out, he didn't really have to go. Another mother was concerned about her son's refusal to participate in an after school sports activity. She wanted to know if she should "make" him attend, or whether it was okay to let him drop out. In both these situations the concern was about giving the message that you can just drop out of something you don't like, or that is hard to do. Parents have expressed that concern about a variety of activities that children may resist doing.

The fact is that these situations are not so clear cut; there are things to consider on all sides. It may seem pointless to try to force a child to do something he has such strong negative feelings about. Also, these negative feelings are usually expressed in behavior that is difficult to deal with. Yet in both these examples the mothers felt the children would benefit greatly, in the one case, by continuing in the nursery program, in the other, by continuing in the sports program. Not only that, but in both instances the mothers reported that the children actually enjoyed participating once there.

There is no "right" answer as such to these dilemmas. So how do you arrive at your own judgment? Actually, you get the information you need by asking *yourself* questions about your child. Using these same examples, the first question would be, what is the reason for the resistance? In both situations, the moms had very clear ideas about what they thought were the reasons, but that was not what they were thinking about. They also were not giving enough credit to their own understanding of their children's behavior. They were focused on what to do about it, rather than on what the children were actually feeling. For one child it was anxiety about performing well enough; for the other it was difficulty with the transition itself from home to school.

Once this was understood, it became possible to think about what could be done to help the children take the steps that were causing them difficulty. The focus shifted from how to "make" them take these steps, to how to help them take these steps. In both instances the parents knew they really believed it best for the children to move forward, even if that was hard. The conflict they felt was about whether their own insistence would somehow be damaging to their children.

We worry that we may somehow harm our children by making mistakes in our judgment. But children are very resilient and can survive many mistakes. Besides, we learn from our mistakes and become better parents as a result.

Perhaps the most important point is to put more trust in our understanding of the meaning of our children's behavior. When our judgment is based on such understanding, our children become our partners. We're not then doing it alone.

SOCIAL PRESSURES

Trust Your Judgment

"SpongeBob Square Pants" has become controversial—again. New research reports that 4-year-olds who had just watched the show, did worse on tests of attention and problem-solving than young children who watched a slower paced educational program or spent time drawing.

This study is not just about "SpongeBob", but is part of an effort to determine the impact of different types of television shows on children rather than the amount of television watched. Setting aside conflicting expert opinions about the validity of this particular study, it has served to provoke renewed—or ongoing—concern about the effect of television viewing on children's development. These days, the hot button question has to do with the impact of television—and the computer, and video games, and smart phones—on the developing brain.

This question, too, is as yet unanswerable since not enough of a time span has elapsed to permit definitive conclusions about changes in the brain due to the newest media. One point of view is that the rapid-fire imagery and fast pacing to which children are exposed is leading to decreased ability to focus and to pay attention. The opposite viewpoint is that the nature of the new media and their content are preparing children's brains to function in the high-tech world in which they will be living.

What I think is as important—or maybe even more important—about this controversy and others, is their impact on parents. Parents increasingly search for "scientific" answers to child-rearing questions. It is not just that parents, of course, want to do the best for their children. It is, rather, the idea that "the best" will be found in the latest theories and scientific research. But is child-rearing a science?

Ever since child development research began to play a major role in our thinking about children, new and changing theories have been promoted. These theories always find their way into popular media translated into prescriptions for parents about how they should raise their children.

If you were a new mother in the 1950's you surely would have been reading Dr. Spock, who, like others, was influenced by psychoanalytic theories. The methods prescribed were supposed to lead to emotionally well-adjusted children.

Next came an emphasis on teaching letters and numbers. The fear was that we were falling behind in science and mothers were supposed to fix that with methods that would make children smart.

In the 1960's, pre-school programs like Headstart and TV programs like Sesame Street were meant to help children who were "culturally deprived." Then in the '70's you might have been sold on the importance of "bonding" in order to insure secure "attachment" between mother and child. And in the "80's came the idea that we could fix sexism by raising our children with politically correct toys and clothes.

All of which brings us most recently, with the advent of research into the developing brain, to instructions we are getting about avoiding harmful effects and promoting that development. It is striking that whatever the problems of the day, the solution always seems to lie in child-rearing. Mothers can fix everything if only they will use the "right" methods in raising their children.

Mothers are bombarded with child-rearing advice and much of it is filled with scary messages: there is a "right" way to do things; you can damage your child if you do things the "wrong" way. What gives all this advice weight is that it is supposedly based on scientific research. Popular magazine covers show babies with electrodes attached to their heads. What could be more scientific!

Modern technology has helped us learn a great deal about the development of the human brain. It is exciting to find out how much more is going on in the first years of life than we ever imagined. The problem is that research that has helped us learn more about *how* children develop, is then used to make prescriptions for bringing about that development. But knowing how something happens doesn't tell us how to make it happen—or how to avoid having it happen.

Many new mothers have told me that the hardest part of new motherhood for them is the feeling of having a new job, with no training, and not knowing what they were doing. Women today, who have had experience in the workplace believe there must be a "right" way of doing things, and if they master the "right" skills for this job of child-rearing they will be successful.

But children and mothers are all individuals who don't fit the prescriptions. Besides, the prescriptions themselves are not science—no matter how it might reassure us to believe they are. So, whether it is a matter of letting your child watch "SpongeBob" or making many other decisions, it comes down to knowing your own child.

The answer does not lie in science. It lies in your own judgment. Use it and trust it!

Entitled?

Do our children feel entitled to have all the things they see around them? A friend who spent Christmas with children and grandchildren was struck by the fact that every gift unwrapped was an ipad, an iphone, an ipod, an electronic game, or something else in the world of technology.

A mother told me that her son had been begging her for an ipad which she was opposed to getting for him. It had become a major area of conflict. Then, at a birthday party she discovered that every boy in his class had an ipad. She felt torn between her own feeling that this was inappropriate and empathy for her son as the only one of his friends not to have one.

Many parents have described this same conflict. Children are bombarded from all sides by alluring "toys". They live in an electronic world in which it seems that exciting new gadgets appear daily. They are taught early on to use the computer in school. There is endless software of mixed value for children, and they play games on the computer at home. Preschool children have their own cell phones.

In many ways play has been commercialized to a new level. Since the early days of television, parents have been struggling with children's exposure to all kinds of games and toys presented as exciting fun. But the conflict parents feel now is more intense for several reasons. One concern is that many of these new "toys" open a world to children that may be inappropriate for their age, or have content of which parents don't approve. Many video games are violent. Children are drawn to the computer for instant messaging instead of homework. The result is many more areas of conflict between parents and children.

A second important reason for parents' concern is that these new "toys" are expensive. Buying an ipad is not the same as stopping at the five and dime store (if there still is any such place) to placate a child who is begging for a new toy. For parents who cannot afford to buy the things children want, the issue is much clearer. That family has greater priorities. Often parents feel inadequate because of their inability to provide these things.

Yet what I hear from many parents, those who have the financial means and those who don't, is a sense of outrage at what they hear as children's demands. They are angry that children seem to feel entitled to have what they want. What is puzzling about this is that children have always thought they should have whatever they want. That is the self-centered nature of childhood, and that is why there have always been conflicts between parents and children. Children want one thing and parents want something different—whether things or behavior.

What seems to be driving this now is the cost of many of these new things, and perhaps the sense that they were not really intended for children. What bothers many parents is children's apparent lack of awareness of, or indifference to the expense involved. The feeling seems to be that children have no right just to expect things of this magnitude, to act as though they have a right—are entitled—to them.

But sometimes I wonder if this is not our own conflict as parents which we want our children to solve for us. It's as if we wish they wouldn't ask so that we wouldn't have to worry about whether it is right or wrong to say yes or no. On the no side, perhaps coming out of our own upbringing, is the feeling that it is just wrong for a child to get so many expensive things. But then on the yes side is the identification with our child wanting to have what the other kids have; our realization that it is a different world out there from the one we may have grown up in.

A big part of the problem lies in thinking there is a right answer. Part of the challenge of being a parent is in having to think these things through again and again. Children grow and mature, which changes the answer. Situations are different, and that changes the answer. Parents have different values, and that changes the answer from one parent to another.

But what can help is to realize that these requests or demands are really no different than the ones children have always made. It always comes back to the same question: How do we help children learn to tolerate frustration, to accept not getting everything they want, to respect parental decisions even when they don't like them. These are the things we have to start teaching from earliest childhood: making our own decisions based on our own values, about when and when not to gratify children's wishes, and helping them deal with their disappointment or anger when they don't get what they want.

This teaching and learning have to begin long before the ipad question rears its head.

Competition

We live in a competitive society which impacts us—and our children—in many ways. A little two and a half year old I was introduced to recently proudly showed off the uniform he was wearing to compete in the "big game" of his soccer league. Children are given more and more tests these days to measure their achievement, compare them to others, and rank them accordingly. Parents feel pressure for their children to achieve in many areas, so they will be advantaged in school, work, and life; children in turn feel that pressure.

People react differently to this pressure to be number one, and to have their children be number one. Some parents look for ways to diminish the influence of competition. Others say they don't like it, but since that's the way it is, they have to be part of it or their children will lose out.

Depending on their own point of view, parents also respond differently to their children. At one extreme is the Chinese Tiger mother who reported tearing up the card her daughter made for her because it wasn't good enough. One of her accusations was that Western mothers are too worried about their children's self-esteem.

I don't know if they are too worried, but parents do get concerned when the constant comparison to others causes children to start questioning their own self-worth. A mother told me about her son's upset when the teacher made a positive comment about another child's paper rather than his. He said that meant his paper wasn't as good.

Good, better, best. How can we help children deal with those gradations when there is so much pressure—sometimes from us—to be the best? The reality is that there are very few people who are the best at everything, and that certainly applies to children as well. The problem is how to help children keep from equating "not the best", with "not good". How can we help them know when they are good, even when they are not the best, and that perhaps they can get better with practice or work.

Here is where we have to get real, both with our children and ourselves. This means acknowledging first to ourselves our children's strengths and weaknesses. Sometimes the idea is conveyed that a child is not so good at something because he or she is not trying, or working hard enough. Other times more emphasis is put on those areas that a child finds more difficult.

This happens a lot with sports. Especially during the growing years, some children seem to be especially well coordinated and natural athletes. Some children hit the home runs and get to be captain while others are the last ones picked for the team. Obviously, this doesn't feel very good, and children often become resistant to sports as a result.

The same is true in other areas of children's lives as they are growing up. Some children are more social, others seem to be natural leaders around whom others gravitate. Some are more creative or musical, others excel in science, or building things. Children themselves are very aware of these differences. At different stages of development certain skills may be more valued in their peer group than others. But if what they are good at is not valued now, they may value their own skills less.

Parents often react in one of two ways—or both ways at different times. One way is to provide more instruction or put emphasis on those areas where a child is not as good as some peers. In some situations that is appropriate and helpful. But another common reaction is to offer reassurance—even insist that a child is just as good as anyone else, or everyone else. The problem is that children don't believe you when you do that and it makes them feel that you "don't get it".

Parents worry that a child will believe he's not good at something and want to reassure him that it's not true. But the fact that the child feels that way is true, no matter what the reality may be. You can validate a child's feeling without validating the fact. It's hard to feel that you are not good at something. Showing an understanding of the feeling is what can open the larger conversation about people being good or best at different things.

The child whose paper had not been singled out had in fact been singled out for praise at other times. Self-esteem comes from an ability to appreciate one's own strengths and skills. Praise for those strengths is more readily valued when it connects with what is real for a child rather than offered to contradict his feelings.

The challenge for us as parents is to help a child become the best that he or she can be—not necessarily better than someone else. That's not easy to do when the pressure all around is to be "the best".

Race To The Top

We've heard that phrase a lot lately. It is the name of the program that gives federal financial awards to those states that make certain changes in their school systems. The goal is to improve the quality of education throughout our country.

Hopefully, children will benefit from these changes.

Will they? Will parents benefit? We don't know the answer to those questions yet, but it sometimes seems that the name itself has had an impact. "Race to the top"; a race is a competition, and top means better than everyone else. But should children who are developing and learning really be in a competition? And can every one of them be at the top? Parents are under a lot of pressure these days to answer, "Yes", and to make just that happen.

It may be useful for States to compete in providing the best education. But the trickle down effect raises many questions. Children do not develop in the same way or at the same time. They can't all be at the top—and certainly not at the same time. Yet getting the best education—whether in private or public schools—seems to be more and more dependent on a competition to be at the top. And parents feel responsible for getting them there.

As parents we have a number of contradictory goals: we want our children to be individuals, to be like everyone else, and also to be better than anyone else. Starting with their youngest years we seem to have the idea that earlier is better. Mothers compare notes on whether children have given up the bottle, are toilet trained, are saying words, or have taken other developmental steps. They are proud when their children are first, and worry if they see differences from other children.

Educators as well as parents, we all seem to have forgotten what we once knew about child development. There is a *range* in the ages at which children achieve developmental milestones. Perhaps even more significantly, there is a *range* of innate differences in personality, temperament, skills, talents and interests among children. This translates into differences in behavior, readiness for specific tasks, and mastery of skills, at points along the way.

Unfortunately, the expectation is that everyone be in the same place at the same time. Of course earlier seems wonderful while later becomes worrisome. Yet both may be very much on course, and both may be true of the same child at different times regarding different skills. Although we think we value individuality, there are too many situations in which we don't apply it.

For example, mothers have often talked to me about their concerns in two areas of behavior in particular, even in very young children. One has to do with physical activity, the other with social ease. Some children have a greater need to use their bodies, to move around more, to explore. They may find it harder to sit still or stay focused on a teacher-centered activity. Too often this leads to thoughts of attention deficit or hyperactivity.

The other worry is about children who may be less expressive or outgoing, particularly in social interactions, or in response to questions—from adults in particular. Mothers are concerned that children will not be able to show what they know, and may be disadvantaged for that, especially in educational settings.

In these examples, as well as others, the worrying often has more to do with our own expectations and wishes than with any "problem" in our child. We sometimes have trouble seeing who our child really is because we have a different image in our minds of who our child should be, or who we want him or her to be. We also may be struggling with conflict between our respect for individuality and the feeling that our child should behave like everyone else. And sometimes that pressure may be coming from the world out there—teachers, grandparents, even other parents.

It is because of these many pressures that the challenge for us as parents is to know, and stay in touch with who our child really is. We need to give recognition to strengths and support where help is needed, without trying to make our child into someone else.

Sometimes we are not aware that our own ambitions and anxieties are often communicated to our children, who then interpret these feelings as a reflection of their own inadequacies or failures. Such feelings don't inspire the very self-confidence we are hoping to give our children. Our children need us as their advocates. Let's be those advocates without pressure to compete in the race to the top.

More Praise For Parents

Once again American students are being compared unfavorably to students from other countries. This time parents, instead of teachers are getting the blame. Thomas Friedman, commenting in the New York Times on a study done by the Program for International Student Assessment concludes that we should stop putting the whole burden on teachers, and that "we need better parents".

Parents are used to being criticized, but in this instance they should be praised instead for the influence they *do* have on their children's educational achievement. This study indicated that students whose parents read to them regularly in their early school years scored markedly higher on the tests that were given. Furthermore, "just asking your child how was their school day and showing genuine interest in the learning they are doing can have the same impact as hours of private tutoring."

It is interesting that reading a book with your children, or talking about things they have done during the day, has a greater impact than just playing with them. One bit of news in a related study that parents may also find interesting, is that being involved with children's learning at home has a greater impact on children's achievement than attending P.T.A and school meetings, volunteering in classrooms or helping with fund raising.

A few days after this newspaper article appeared stressing the importance of reading to your children, another article reported that parents are rejecting children's e-books. Even parents who use Kindles and iPads for their own reading want old-fashioned print books for their children. According to the article, "parents also say they like cuddling up with their child and a book, and fear that a shiny gadget might get all the attention". This quote reflects several important distinctions between digital reading and paper books.

On a plane during my holiday travel, a little boy who seemed about four years old was "reading" a Dr. Seuss book on an ipad. The illustrations were sharp and the colors bright, but what seemed really to capture his attention was turning the pages. With a flourish he made large sweeping motions in an exaggeration of the method used on Apple products. This was so captivating for him that he barely looked at each page.

Even more startling, on the return flight was a baby about nine months old with both her parents. As the mom was fixing up their seats, dad held the little girl over his shoulder facing a movie screen right behind him. There was no movie at that point and on the screen was a still picture of individual panels with a picture in each. The baby kept reaching over to touch one of the panels and seemed puzzled that nothing was happening. It may have been my imagination, but it clearly seemed that she had experienced touching her parent's iphone or ipad and expected that her touch would change the picture.

The point is that the digital experience for children is something quite different than what we think of as reading to our children. Parents do get that. I saw the little boy with the ipad later, cuddled up against his mother who was reading a book to him. Together they pointed to, and talked about some of the things in the illustrations. It was not hard to see that this reading experience would make a more meaningful and lasting impression than turning the pages of an ipad.

The first newspaper article emphasized the intellectual benefits of reading to children, while the parents in the second article are focused on the emotional component. When children keep wanting "one more book" at bedtime, which often turns into three or four more, of course they like to hear the stories. But what they are really holding onto is that special up-close and personal time with mom or dad. These are the warm feelings that become attached to the experience of reading and that stay with children later on.

An educator quoted in the article also talks about how the shape and size of books are often part of the reading experience. Width and height of books help to convey their content. Size and shape "become part of the emotional experience, the intellectual experience". The joining together of the emotional and intellectual experience is the key.

It is the emotional experience of reading to our children, and later on showing an interest in their school work that helps shape their intellectual experience and development. The two are joined. Parents worry at times about teaching colors, letters, numbers. But children are learning this as part of what parents are already doing by reading to them.

I disagree with Tom Friedman. We need to praise parents for what they do so well, and for the influence they have. Parents are not told this often enough.

Too Many Virtues

A good friend calls my attention now and then to articles on topics she thinks might interest my readers, or that I might want to write about. The most recent is a review of a book called, "Will Power" which deals with self-control. Along with intelligence, self-control was thought to be the best predictor of success in life. Except, as I wrote last week, "grit", or perseverance now seems to have taken the lead.

In the book review, the reviewer refers to a well known experiment in which preschoolers were given a choice in which they could have one marshmallow they could eat right away; but if they waited fifteen minutes (I thought it was ten) until the examiner returned before eating it, they could have two marshmallows. The one marshmallow was on a plate in front of the child, so he had to see it without eating it. (Ouch!) These children were followed up many years later and it was found that the 4-year-olds who waited for two marshmallows were more successful in all kinds of ways.

It seems to me that a case could be made that a bird in the hand is worth two in the bush, which might lead to a different kind of success. And some things won't taste that good if you let them sit too long. But the book in question is focused on the importance of self-control, and gives lots of advice on how to build up willpower.

Thinking about this, and the topics of some of my recent posts, what I see is the possibility of parents taking away from them too many do's and don'ts. Don't let your children watch "SpongeBob", it can be bad for their attention and problem-solving abilities. Gratifying children is bad, because frustration helps develop "grit". And now, make your children wait, because that will develop self-control.

Unfortunately, that is often the outcome of some of the reporting on these well-intentioned studies. The problem is that will-power, self-control, enduring deprivation or frustration, all start to seem like moral virtues, as though indicating a "good" or "bad" child. It is as though these virtues are somehow ends in themselves, having nothing to do with real people or the realities of life.

Ideas like these were part of the early history of childhood, when "breaking the will" was considered an essential means of raising "good" children. In more recent times we believed that picking up a crying child would spoil him. And not that long ago there were rigid schedules for feeding babies, with the idea that feedings every four hours, no matter how they cried, would teach them to wait.

We learned in time that the harsh methods of teaching these virtues also taught children less desirable ideas and feelings about life and relationships with others. Then, as now, research in child development led to changing directions in child-rearing. We went on to demand feeding, to the importance of children expressing themselves, to meeting children's needs. At times it almost seems as though we went from *children* should be seen and not heard, to *parents* should be seen and not heard.

But I get worried when we seem to be moving back to "virtues", or in this case, supposed characteristics of success, instead of thinking about our children themselves. Yes, self-control is important, because we can't just hit someone if we're angry. Tolerating frustration is important, because we can't always get what we want the minute we want it. Will-power is important, because it helps us do our homework when we would rather talk to our friends.

The point is that it's hard to wait for that cookie—sometimes even if you know you'll get two if you wait. The ability to use self-control, to tolerate frustration, is something that grows as part of development. As parents, we play a role in that development through our expectations and support. We no longer expect babies to wait to be fed. At the same time, we do gradually begin to modify their feedings somewhat to help them begin to move closer to day/night distinctions and eventually to three meals a day.

Hopefully, we make these changes not according to some rigid formula, but by getting to know our own baby. We make adjustments using our own judgment, based on feedback we get from our baby's behavior. In the same way, as our children grow we can appreciate their struggles in mastering frustration and developing self-control. Their behavior tells us that something is hard for them, not that they are "bad", or deficient in some way.

Our goal as parents needs to be to support children who are having a hard time learning to wait or to use self-control, not to try to make them do this in the service of developing "grit". We can be supportive by showing that we understand when something is hard, and by helping them gain mastery through our words, our reassurance, and at times just going through hard times with them.

Life itself provides many opportunities for children to learn these skills. Teaching them does not require preaching about them as if they were virtues.

How Much Is Too Much?

A discussion seems to be going on in educational circles about whether kids today are experiencing too much pressure—with particular reference to homework. There appear to be conflicting ideas circulating about appropriate expectations of young people and whether they are being subjected to excessive pressure and stress.

On one side, we hear about "race to the top" as creating too much emphasis on tests and leading teachers to "teach to the test", rather than educating in a more meaningful way. On the other hand, we find articles (I discussed one recently) bemoaning the fact that children are being overprotected from anything stressful and as a result are not developing the ability needed to overcome difficulties and frustration in reaching desired goals.

Now a newspaper article reports on "elite" schools concerned about the detrimental effects of over-programming students, rethinking their demands about tests, papers and homework assignments. Parents seem to be of two minds about this. Some parents see hard work in school as essential to making their children competitive. A father is quoted saying it was unlikely that parents in India and China were fretting about overwork.

Other parents feel it is counterproductive for their children to be up half the night studying, expressing concern about the health effects of stress and sleep deprivation. Another father is quoted as saying, "There's no value in stressing kids out. You are robbing them of their childhood."

One of our own readers commented, "It's good to get kids into the habit of devoting some time to study each day, even from an early age. But it seems we are overloading them already with too much expectation . . . . Some is good, but how do you decide what is enough?" This question is so important and really gets to the heart of the matter, because a question relating to expectation speaks to so many issues in raising our children.

All along the developmental road we are always asking how much is reasonable and how much is too much to expect. Is it too much to expect her to dress herself, to come into meals when called, to go to bed without a fuss? Is it reasonable to expect him to share his toys, to stop hitting his brother, to clean up his room? Later on these questions get raised about watching TV, about time spent on Facebook, and about doing homework, among other things.

I confronted the complexity of this question recently as it was raised by parents of an eight year old who had started in a new school. The teacher, who seems excellent in many ways, has high expectations and uses several strategies in getting children to meet them. One of these is having children miss recess or snack time to complete work not finished during class time. The parents were concerned because the child, who is very bright, also has been found to need more time to complete some academic tasks even when applying herself appropriately. This kind of difficulty is well-known enough so that there is actually a school procedure in place for allowing more time in test situations.

The parents felt that the child was in effect being punished for a real difficulty and that this might have an effect on her feelings about school, about learning, and about her own abilities. On the other hand, this child had progressed by leaps and bounds since being in this class, was making new friends, and seemed very interested in everything new she was learning. She did not enjoy missing recess and snack a few times, but she did not seem unduly distressed about it. The question was, did the child make the kind of strides she clearly had made *because* of the teachers expectations and methods of implementing them, or in spite of them?

This is the question educators and parents struggle with. So you have the Tiger Mom approach on one side, and a different kind of concern about children's develpment on the other. Which leads back to the reader's question, "How do you decide what is enough?" Does it have to be either extreme, or is it possible to find some balance between the two?

In this, as in so many other situations that involve our children, there is no way of knowing with certainty what the "perfect" or right approach is for each child. In the example I gave, the teacher's method was not one the child had been exposed to before. Yet whatever one thinks of her method, the clarity and consistency of her expectations seemed to have a positive effect on this child's learning and overall adjustment.

Ultimately, to answer questions about expectation we have to use what we know about our own child. We have to learn what we need to know from our children's reactions and behavior. And then, without being too readily put off by a negative response, be willing to adjust our expectations accordingly. Answering how much is too much is a work in progress.

The Blame Game

Why is it that articles that are supposed to be helpful to parents so often end up making you feel terrible about yourself? I just read an article titled, "How to Land Your Kid in Therapy", which really could have been subtitled "Ten Ways to Screw Up Your Kids". It is basically a summary of everything mothers today are doing wrong in raising their children.

The actual subtitle of this article from Atlantic magazine is, "Why the obsession with our kids' happiness may be dooming them to unhappy adulthoods." Although it starts out with the idea that some of the unhappiness in young adults may be due to their parents having been too "good"—caring, understanding, supportive—much of what follows is a discussion of all the bad things mothers do in the service of their children's happiness.

It always interests and amazes me that mothers are held responsible for whatever seems to be troublesome in our society. Mothers are the cause of—and are supposed to fix through child-rearing—whatever is wrong. I pointed out in an earlier post that among other things mothers have been blamed in the past for widespread neuroses, academic failures, failures of attachment, and even gender discrimination. Now the issue seems to be that the sole goal and focus in raising children has become happiness. By leaving out the "pursuit" in the pursuit of happiness, children never have to struggle and are therefore unable to cope when they experience adversity.

I certainly agree that mothers are very invested in their children's happiness. Many times in discussions with mothers about concerns they may have about a child, what I hear is, "I just want her to be happy". It is also the case that if happiness is so all important, any sign that a child is unhappy becomes very worrisome. Probably we all do things that may not really be in our children's best interest if we're too worried about whether or not they are happy.

But the question I want to raise is why are mothers being blamed for the negative consequences of this over investment in happiness? The idea that you are supposed to feel happy all the time is a widespread cultural attitude. Happiness has become an entitlement. If you are not happy, that means something is wrong. Even while writing this, an ad came up on the computer showing a beautiful young woman lying in bed with the heading, "I'm not sad, but I'm not happy either". The attached article would tell you how to fix that.

I heard a talk recently on the enormous increase in pharmacotherapy-treatment with psychotropic drugs. The interesting fact is that the greatest numbers of prescriptions are written by general medical practioners, not psychiatrists. Also, the drugs are being prescribed for the most part not for mental illness but for a wide variety of other complaints, including those that could come under the heading of "unhappiness". Clearly, we are all surrounded by the idea that we are not supposed to feel any discomfort, and that pills are available to make us feel "happy".

More specifically, those of us who are the supposed "experts" in child development need to take some responsibility for the anxiety mothers feel about their children, and the concern about "happiness" that this can lead to. Ever since the advent of child development research, mothers have been warned about all the things that can go awry as our children grow, and all the things they are supposed to do to prevent that from happening.

The whole idea of "meeting children's needs", so prominent in much child guidance material, is in practice a murky matter. What is a need as opposed to a want? Is it bad to gratify children, harmful to frustrate them? If a child is upset, withdrawn, angry, does that mean there is a problem, that we as parents have done something wrong? It is not surprising that mothers use happiness as the measure of whether their children are well adjusted, and of their own success as parents.

We live at a time when family members live at great distances from one another. As a result, many families are without a much needed support system in raising their children. The economy is such that too often both parents have to work, whether they want to or not. Child-rearing practices that at one time were handed down from one generation to the next are no longer considered valid. We reject our own parents' advice, sometimes because we don't like the way we turned out, but also because of the widespread idea that child-rearing is a science which requires an expert. Child guidance manuals promote that idea.

The fact is, children are always going to dislike what parents expect of them. Giving up childish pleasures in order to become a social being is not easy. Children are going to feel angry, frustrated and unhappy at times in the process. They blame their parents for that. Why are we joining them in the blame game?

CPSIA information can be obtained at www.ICGtesting.com
Printed in the USA
BVOW011205131112

305432BV00001B/6/P